Life in the Fast Brain

by

Karen L. J. Isaacson

Gifted Unlimited, LLC

Life in the Fast Brain

Cover Design: Hutchison-Frey
Interior Design: The Printed Page
Copy Editor: Jen Ault

Printed on recycled paper

Published by
Gifted Unlimited, LLC
12340 U.S. Hwy. 42 #453
Goshen, KY, 40026
www.giftedunlimitedllc.com

Printed and bound in the United States of America

First Edition

11 10 09 08 07   6 5 4 3 2 1

Library of Congress Cataloging-in-Publication Data

Isaacson, Karen L. J., 1965-
Life in the fast brain / by Karen L.J. Isaacson.
p. cm.
ISBN-13: 978-0-910707-82-4
ISBN-10: 0-910707-82-0
1. Gifted persons—Psychology. 2. Genius. 3. Creativity. I. Title.
BF412.I83 2007
305.9'089—dc22
2007035958

ISBN-13: 978-0-910707-82-4
ISBN-10: 0-910707-82-0

Dedication

To my best friend, Len.

Acknowledgments

I want to give a big thanks (as well as a big hug) to my husband, children, parents, and siblings for being good sports and allowing me to share some of their most embarrassing moments with the rest of the world. Not only have they made this book possible, they've made my own life, ahem, *interesting*.

Contents

 # Characters

I've listed the names of my family members who appear in this book according to their place in the family. All names have been changed to mask their identities. Besides, their real names are boring.

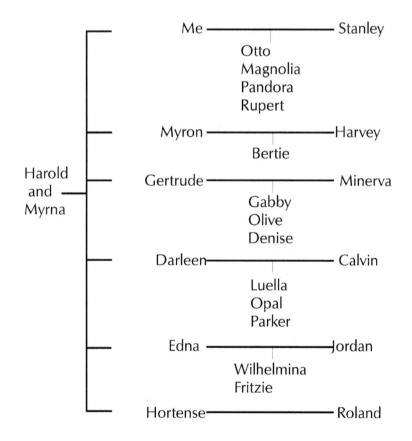

Me ——————— Stanley
> Otto
> Magnolia
> Pandora
> Rupert

Myron ——————— Harvey
> Bertie

Harold and Myrna

Gertrude ——————— Minerva
> Gabby
> Olive
> Denise

Darleen ——————— Calvin
> Luella
> Opal
> Parker

Edna ——————— Jordan
> Wilhelmina
> Fritzie

Hortense ——————— Roland

# Preface

This book is for anyone who lives with or knows gifted kids or adults, or who is gifted him- or herself. Like my earlier book, *Raisin' Brains*, it's an inside look at giftedness. There are fewer stories about my mom this time. That's because she seems more and more normal to me as I grow older and experience many of the things that she went through.

Uh oh. That statement concerns me on two counts. One: Why am I becoming more and more immune to her eccentricities? Is it because I am developing a few of my own? Two: I don't think I really want to experience many of the things that she went through as a mother, because she didn't have an easy job of it.

While my first book focused heavily on my oldest three children, this book focuses more on the youngest two, Pandora and Rupert. Stanley and Otto have both graduated from high school and have moved on to college and jobs. And since Magnolia is currently busy being a teenager (my husband and I are hoping that each of our children eventually move beyond this stage and that we'll live to tell the tale), she appears less often in the following pages.

Pandora is now a pre-teen but has yet to surrender herself to complete conformity.

That leaves Rupert, who, at seven, has the freshest brain, least spoiled by society's norms. I love observing a fast brain in its natural, yet-to-be-fully-socialized habitat. What's so great about Rupert is that he is standing on the edge of the proverbial mold and has yet to be pressed into place by the words and hands-on training of well-meaning adults.

1: On the Bright Side

Life in the fast brain—whether it's your brain or someone else's—brings both blessings and curses, as most people who live with such a brain well know.

But if you don't have personal experience (and I suspect many of you do), just try to imagine what it's like for a person whose every thought is at an intellectually higher speed than the majority of those around him or her. Warp speed. Yikes! How does that person cope with the rest of the world? And even more important, how does the world cope with that person?

When the Wright brothers had a dream that other people thought was crazy, they ignored the rest of the world, and in spite of scorn and disbelief, they went right on dreaming and fiddling with their dream until it had wings to soar. I have a feeling that they were probably not easy guys to live with during those dream-chasing days. They must have experienced a good bit of frustration when the rest of the world took so long to appreciate the value of their work. But at least they had each other. They had sympathetic intensity.

Intellectual intensity brings *delight* with the discovery of new concepts, and *frustration* and *isolation* if and when you can't communicate those concepts to others. It's like living in a world of people who speak a different language and who don't have similar life experiences. There is nothing on which to base a relationship and no one who can understand your thoughts. Imagine having a brilliant idea explode in your mind—an epiphany—that you want to share with someone. The idea that a machine could be made that could fly! Then, when you attempt to tell others about it, you get nothing but blank stares and disbelief, sometimes even scorn.

Few others understood the dream or thought that the Wright brothers had any hope of ever making a flying machine. And imagine Galileo's frustration with those who could not accept the idea that the earth revolved around the sun!

I am intensely creative. My brain can't be compared to Galileo's (no way), but it does like to think unusual thoughts nonetheless. Personally, I find that a creative opportunity is better than a vacation. My brain loves nothing more than running ahead and reorganizing ideas or materials into something new and different. But I do wish other people could understand. I wish they didn't expect me to do things their way—to, oh, you know, pay bills and be responsible and fit in with the rest of society and all of that.

Creative gifts can bring intense pleasure in the act of creating. They also bring pain, as when creations are less than perfect or are misunderstood. A creative person can visualize an outcome in his mind, and then, when reality falls short of this ideal, it is easy to get discouraged. An artist or a musician may create a masterpiece—she may use her medium to throw out her most sacred thoughts to the world with the hope that she will connect with someone who will understand what she is trying to say. Then, when others don't comprehend or appreciate her creation, she may feel alone and rejected.

People with creative brains are often very sensitive. Increased sensitivity brings both intense joy and intense pain, as your senses react to every experience on a physical or emotional level, or both. I have a friend who meets every experience with an intensified reaction. She is a delight to be around when good things are happening, but if someone squashes a bug, her heart breaks. This is difficult for others to understand, and they may believe that her pain is dramatized rather than real and deeply felt. But it's real. How does she manage to be around people who think she is acting when those are, in fact, her true feelings?

A person with a fast brain—whether that brain is creative, or extra sensitive, or extra intellectually intense—needs coping skills to handle feelings of disappointment, failure, or inability to share his or her passion with others.

Everyone needs coping skills. No matter who you are or what you do, life has a way of coming at you with unexpected sucker punches. Things happen. If you factor in family members or work colleagues, including those who have a good dose of divergent thinking, intense passion, perfectionism, asynchronous development, and sensitivity—all common traits of people with runaway brains—you have quite a mix to cope with! You have to be on your toes. You have to be in your own fast brain.

As a mother of five children, I have developed some good coping skills. I have also developed some highly creative coping skills. Whether I'm hunting down the source of an unidentified water-operated contraption-in-progress that is about to take over the bathroom sink area, or stopping a child's "*Why?*" in its tracks, I have learned to keep a good supply of coping tools handy.

While there isn't anything terribly original about looking at the bright side, I have found it to be one of my best sanity savers. It beats counting backwards from 10 and taking deep breaths. It even beats a big bowl of ice cream, though I must admit I do indulge in a little comfort food now and then, when optimism alone isn't enough to do the trick. It's important not to rely too heavily on just one technique for dealing with difficulty; you could develop immunities. But I am willing to test the immunity theory if it has to do with ice cream.

By now, you may be picturing me weighing in at 500 pounds and living in La La Land, blissfully ignoring both the bathroom scale and problems that spring up like dandelions. But no, it doesn't work that way. Not with the kind of coping skills I'm referring to.

For coping with any kind of stress, there are a lot of opportunities available—you know, things like golfing, jogging, therapeutic advice, hitting a punching bag, shopping, and really lo-o-ong vacations. Everyone has a few favorites. I'm sure you have yours.

But for an easy, reliable, you-can-always-count-on-it recipe for coping, my favorite strategy is looking on the bright side, or the lighter side. I have lots of other strategies, which I will talk about in later chapters, but looking at the bright side comes first. Why? Because it gives me hope. Look at that. "Hope" rhymes with "cope." Not that *that* has anything to do with anything, but hey, it's a cool coincidence.

When you're a fast brain yourself, it's more important than ever to be able to look on the bright side of things and to envision the positive. It may not change the situation, but it puts your mind in a less stressful position and enables you to think more clearly, or to at least enjoy what there is to enjoy without having all of the sunshine blocked out by the clouds.

Recently, on a Monday morning, when I was volunteering at our elementary school, a sixth-grade teacher walked into the faculty lounge to get some coffee. He looked a little frazzled. "I must be losing my marbles," he said. "I just finished teaching an English lesson, and after I finished, my students told me I gave that same lesson last Friday."

"Wow," I thought. But then, "Oh, well," my coping brain said out loud, without much advance thinking. "Look at it this way: The good news is that at least they were paying attention on Friday."

His face lit up. "You know what? You're right!" He seemed much happier with that thought.

I must say that kind of positive spin doesn't always work. The other day I was speaking with a friend who had gone away for the weekend with her husband and returned home only to find that her teenage son had hosted a party at their home—a party with all of the traditional teenage accompaniments, like alcohol and police cars. My friend was devastated. When someone asked her if her house was trashed, she said, "Oh no. He made sure he put all of the valuable and breakable stuff away."

I jumped in with, "Well, the good news is that he was responsible enough to do that."

She gave me one of those looks that could kill. Apparently, this wasn't the right time or place for looking at the bright side. So keep that in mind.

I don't think that my friend was emotionally ready for the "hope" stage. Her mind was still reeling from shock and worry. Sometimes we have to work through things a bit before we can jump into the hope business. However, the sixth-grade teacher was another story. When he realized that his class was actually listening, he had hope, because that meant all he had to do was get it together himself. He was having a bad day. It was temporary.

Hope is a magical thing. It keeps you going when nothing else will. It's the only thing that gives the impossible a shot at life. It fuels our dreams.

▦ ▦ ▦

We have some friends who dug a big hole in their backyard for a duck pond. Then they added a paddle boat and a dock, and my youngest two children were very impressed. However, what my nine-year-old Pandora and six-year-old Rupert didn't realize is that our friends had hired guys with backhoes to dig the pond.

So when we got home, Pandora and Rupert began scheming. They wanted a pond in our backyard—also a boat and a dock. The very next day, they began digging—with shovels. As I watched them dig, *I* knew their task was overwhelming, but *they* didn't know that. So they kept digging. I didn't stop them. I didn't tell them that their goal was next to impossible. You need to know that where we live, we don't have normal soil; we have rocks and clay, but mostly rocks. Digging is difficult work, even for an adult. You might describe digging in our backyard more accurately as "very slow, metal-induced erosion."

After a full day's worth of digging, Pandora and Rupert finally achieved a hole about the size of a mud puddle. When their dad came home from work, they asked him to help. After a few hours with a pick axe, the three of them had a hole that was about eight feet long and six inches deep. If it had been full of water, a person could have laid down in it and gotten wet on one side. It was a far cry from a pond with a dock and a boat. At that rate, my great-grandchildren will have to finish the job. It'll be a long-term family project. I have a feeling I'll never live to see the boat rides.

But Pandora and Rupert woke up the next morning and worked happily all day long, dreaming about being pirates and discussing which friends would be invited over to swim and build forts on the prime real estate overlooking the beach. Even though they were only removing a few spoonfuls of clay at a time, they had hope. They had something grand that they could envision, and it made them happy to make progress toward that goal.

When I get discouraged with things, I keep reminding myself that it's the progress that matters—even if it's only an inch at a time.

I think about that pond often. When I'm struggling with a highly intelligent teenager who refuses to believe that she really *is* intelligent, or a perfectionist daughter who feels that "good enough" is a far cry from adequate, or a little boy whose imagination carries him far away into a world of space engineering instead of the world of reading where his classroom teacher expects him to be, I feel like I'm trying to solve the problem with a hand trowel instead of a backhoe. The situation is overwhelming. I have to step back and say, "You know, progress is progress. At least we're moving in the right direction."

As a parent, I don't have the luxury of giving up, like Pandora and Rupert eventually did on the pond—at least until the next summer, when they once again envisioned a small lake with a sunken ship or a hidden sea monster. I have to keep going, keep supporting my kids, whatever the issues of the moment may be.

Looking at the bright side is what keeps me going, keeps me believing that everything will turn out all right, that there is hope. Problems can be resolved. A sensitive child *will* eventually find a peer who can understand his deep and intense feelings and empathize with him. A scattered child who is capable of succeeding everywhere but finds satisfaction nowhere *will* eventually find a happy spot to land. It *can* happen. We just have to get there a shovel-full, or maybe a spoonful, at a time.

It saves my sanity, just knowing that we're making progress.

⊞　⊞　⊞

Sometimes, being gifted means that you have the ability to better understand or comprehend the seriousness of a situation or the possible consequences. You have access to more information and can visualize a variety of outcomes. It's just like parents whose experience allows them to more correctly assess a situation than their children might, and whose sense of responsibility demands that they attempt to avoid undesirable outcomes.

When I was in third grade and lived in north Idaho, our town was hit one spring with a deluge of rain. The snow melted too fast, and the rain came down too quickly. The river was rising rapidly. In the middle of the day, the school decided it had better send us kids home or it might be stuck with us for a week, or who knew how long, and nobody wanted that. So, full of enthusiasm and gratitude for a little excitement in our otherwise mundane lives, we hopped on our respective buses and headed home for an unexpected vacation. My family lived up the North Fork, and I watched with a funny feeling in my stomach as the river water lapped at the edge of the road. I wondered if the bus would make it back to the schoolyard.

Shortly after we got home from school, the neighbors who lived on lower ground grabbed their kids and evacuated before their houses washed away. My dad was out of town, so my mom was alone with four children, one of them a baby.

She called my dad and said, "You'd better get home right now, or you might not get home at all."

"Don't worry. It's just a little high water." My dad is always the optimist.

Just minutes later, the roads washed out completely, and our home, which was at the base of a hillside, became part of a virtual island, as we were surrounded by water on three sides.

That night, my mom said, "Kids, I think we'd better pack some bags. We may have to move higher up the hill."

How cool was that? I'd watched episode after episode of *Gilligan's Island*, and I'd read *My Side of the Mountain* (about a young boy surviving alone in the wilderness), and I realized that this flood might be my chance to live my dream. My younger brother Myron was just as excited as I was. He and I both raced off and packed our necessities, which consisted mostly of toys, because, of course, toys would be the one thing we would need in the wilderness. For Pete's sake, we had plenty of water, we knew how to build a shelter—we were in a constant fort-building mode—and we could live off the land.

My mother was not in agreement. She made us dump the toys and pack boring but practical things like clothes and toothbrushes.

As it turned out, we never did move higher up the hill. The water stopped rising five feet from our house. My dad was flown by helicopter to the top of the hill, and he hiked down to help us. We were stranded without electricity and clean water for weeks. We had to cook dinner in our fireplace.

My brother and I were having the time of our lives.

Our parents, on the other hand, were probably pretty stressed out. Who could blame them? As kids, we were too inexperienced to realize the seriousness of the situation. All we could see was the fun and the fantasy of it. My parents' view of the situation was less rosy. Survival is a critical thing, and when you have four young children depending on you, well, that's a lot of pressure to survive. Our parents had to worry about things like diapers, clean clothing, clean water, heat, and losing a freezer's worth of food because we couldn't eat it fast enough. With their life experience, they were in a better position to assess the seriousness of the situation than we kids were.

▦ ▦ ▦

Advanced learners with fast and efficient brains are often in the same position. A person who is creatively or intellectually gifted has the ability to imagine a million different scenarios, most of them bad or at least undesirable. They think about and worry about all sorts of things. We all want to avoid the undesirable and the unpleasant, but when that's most of what you see, it can get a little overwhelming.

On the other hand, because fast brains can also see so many good possibilities, they can see how the world should be or could be, in terms of betterment, and how it often doesn't measure up to what it could be. Why are people sometimes mean to each other? Why do hunger and poverty still exist in the middle of so much abundance? Why haven't we solved water pollution? We may know what we need to do to fix it, and when the rest of the world doesn't "get it," this can be discouraging to idealistic fast brains.

I understand intellectual frustrations—mostly from the other side of the coin. I feel like such a doofus when I have to call on "technical help" to explain to me once again how to upload my website the hard way, because somehow I have messed up the easy way. I want to ask them to send me instructions in layperson terms, and by that I mean in crayon and with lots of pictures. It is probably frustrating for them, too. They have information for me, but my brain isn't currently equipped to handle it.

Imagine what it's like for the person whose every thought is at an intellectually higher speed than the majority of those around her. How does that person manage?

It's probably why Bill Gates dropped out of college to go do his own thing. It is my understanding that he didn't go to many classes, and he didn't ever crack open a book until right before the final. Thirty years later, Harvard granted him an honorary degree.

⊞ ⊞ ⊞

My children are all at different stages in life. They each have different gifts, quirks, shortcomings, and needs. How do I handle their differences? I often ask myself this question. Often.

There are some days when I feel as though I'm simply reliving a replay of the same nightmare. I wake up, I attempt to wake the children, I run through every vocabulary word that could possibly mean "hurry" followed by "You're going to miss the bus!" Rupert can never find his shoes, even though I remind him daily to always put them away in the same spot. Pandora never has pants to wear, because she is forever growing out of them. Magnolia seems to be permanently installed in the bathroom saying, "Okay, just a minute!" every 10 minutes as I try to convince her that being on time just once would really make me proud.

To be fair, I'm sure my children are asking their friends how to deal with *me*.

Rupert has a natural gift for seeing the bright side of life. He finds sunshine in the most unexpected places. When he lost his first tooth, he thought it was pretty cool. He could blow bubbles with his teeth clenched, and does life get any better than that? I have to marvel at how much this son of mine enjoys life. The little calamities that strike are real and painful to him, but his enthusiasm for trivial blessings, his ability to appreciate little things, is huge. When he was in kindergarten, I bought him a pair of Spiderman snow boots. His gratitude knew no bounds. He showed everyone—kids at school, strangers in the grocery store, everyone. How could I top that?

But, as excited as he was about those boots, it was nothing compared to the black knit snow hat that I fished out of the closet for him to wear to school one morning. I handed it to him, prepared for an argument, but instead, he shouted, "For *me*?" He couldn't believe my generosity. He put it on. "It fits!"

He began dancing around the room and landed in front of a mirror. He pulled the hat over his head. "Look, Mom, I'm a ninja!" Then he pulled it up to a point, "Hey, Mom, do I look like an elf?" He became a leprechaun, a nutcracker, and an obscure movie character, and everything was punctuated by exclamation points. That ordinary little hat provided him with two full days of entertainment, and now, a year later, he still loves that thing. I'm thinking that for his birthday, I should skip the toys and get him a package of socks or something.

Rupert loves everything. He loves school, he loves his hat, and he loves being a ninja, though the only thing he knows about the ancient practice of Japanese martial arts is that ninjas look really cool, dress really cool, and they have really cool numchuks. The other day, when I dropped him off in front of the elementary school, I watched him do a little dance all the way up the sidewalk. He twirled and shook his hips. He didn't care that all of the other parents and kids were watching him; he probably wasn't even aware of their presence. In his own little sunshiny world, they didn't exist.

I watch Rupert, and I learn. Life is good. Yeah, sure, it stinks sometimes, too, but what are you going to do about it?

My dad always told me to skip the worry business. Fix what you can, and don't obsess about what you can't. I've concluded that my dad was right.

Pandora is a perfectionist, but the good news is that she works hard. My young adult son Otto is sensitive in a way that causes him pain sometimes, but the good part of that is that he has developed a deep empathy for others. My oldest son, Stanley, is different from anyone I have ever met, and he has great difficulty finding a place where he fits, but the good news is that when he does find that fit, he will know he is irreplaceable—no one else can do what he does.

Fifteen-year-old Magnolia is stubborn enough to drive two parents crazy. She doesn't understand (or perhaps I mean she doesn't accept) the meaning of the word "no." She will find a way around it somehow. If she wants a thing, even if it's a thing that we cannot afford, she will work on us and work on us until we break down into quivering heaps of jello, submissive to her every whim.

The good news is that she shares my dream that it would be really cool to live in a small Victorian mansion with secret rooms and secret passageways. I, however, as a responsible (while still retaining my sense of the fantastic) adult, know that this is an unrealistic goal, considering our financial means, so I sit back and watch Magnolia at work. She picks up copies of real estate magazines to see what kind of prices we're looking at, and she estimates the value of our own home, should we decide to sell. She does her research online. She develops financial plans to make it all feasible, even though she is blissfully lacking other specific information about what we can afford.

I quietly watch and wait to see if my husband will cave in to her. She has probably met her match on this one, but I can still dream.

The other good news about Magnolia's stubbornness and refutation is that, if it is channeled properly, it can be renamed persistence and determination. When she finally settles on something that she wants badly enough, whether it's an education (ahem, that would be a good goal), a career, or some other goal, she won't stop until she gets it. Forget the shovel; she'll go after it with a backhoe.

As a mom with these five different progeny, I have a great need for focusing on the positive. When I falter in this attempt, my children help me out. When a report card doesn't look so great, Magnolia will say, "But look, Mom. I got an A in art!" If Rupert has swept all of his junk under his bed instead of cleaning his room, he'll say, "But my closet is clean!"

I admit to them that I am grateful for the good stuff, but now we need to work on accomplishing the next good thing, like turning in homework—or even doing the homework in the first place. It's not so much about seeing the light at the end of the tunnel; it's about seeing sparks along the way that remind you that light still exists.

⊞   ⊞   ⊞

When I'm in the middle of chaos, when I'm struggling to find a way to reach a child, I often hear the immortal words of Lennie in *Of Mice and Men*, "Tell me about the rabbits, George." And I remember the importance of my dreams.

Sometimes I, too, need to hear about the rabbits, and no, I'm not speaking of the invisible family of rabbits that Magnolia lived with before she came to our family. I'm referring to those golden specks of Utopian visions that I cling to, knowing all the while that they never will exist in a permanent state. Sure, we'll eventually find our way out of one problem, but another one will always crop up. That's life, no matter what speed your brain is running on. But I need to know that there will be moments of sunshine, and so when I feel a ray on my shoulders, no matter how small, I've got to appreciate it for what it is.

Like Rupert and the old and faded black knit hat, I've got to learn to see the beauty in every little thing. I've got to dream. When it comes to hopes and dreams, Rupert is my hero.

Dreams are the bright side, too. Dreams are the brain's way of envisioning life at its best. Perhaps halfway between our current life and our dreams, we can find an ideal that works in the real world.

Rupert woke up one morning and said, "Mom, do you want to know about my dream that I hope will come true?"

"Sure. Tell me."

"Well, I dreamed I had five buses to hold all of my soldiers and butlers and a huge mansion with five indoor pools and water slides going down underneath each window."

I listened to Rupert sit there and tell me about his "rabbits." From the look on his face, I could tell that this had been a very excellent dream. But of course, I had to be the practical one. I said, "That sounds really cool, but it's going to cost a lot of money. How will you pay for all of that?"

Not to worry. Rupert had it all figured out. "Well, I'm going to have 50 stores, and they will all send me money."

"Yes, dear, but it costs money to open up stores. Where will you get the money to do that?"

He shrugged. "I guess I'll have to marry a rich wife."

Lovely. We went through a similar experience with Otto, at about nine years of age, when he announced that he was going to stay at home and can peaches while his wife went to work. I don't know where my boys are getting this. Certainly my husband didn't marry a rich wife or stay home to can peaches. I think I will blame it on the schools—you know, all those female teachers. Yes, that'll work. Add that to my list of things to blame on the schools. How convenient.

Anyway, it seems that no matter what kind of pitiful reasons I throw at Rupert to be more realistic about his dreams, he shrugs them off. Facts do not weigh him down. He can clearly see the vision of what he wants. Obstacles are just things you toss out of the way.

He's always been like that. When he was five, he wanted to make his own Harry Potter movie. This time, Magnolia was the squelcher. She said, "You can't do that, Rupert. It'll cost millions of dollars. Where are you going to get the money?"

Rupert appeared a little while later with papers in hand. He showed me his designs for a robotic car, which resembled a high-tech chariot with a gun. He had a pile of plans, including an aerial view of the railroad tracks that this new car would require. "I'm going to sell it to the army," he said, "and then I'll use the money from that to pay for my movie."

I said, "That's pretty neat, but you know what? The army already has a lot of transportation. What's special about your car that will make them want to buy it?"

"Don't worry. My robotic car will be faster than anything the army has now. Besides, it will have cup holders with metal sheets to keep the wind from blowing the cups over."

Cup holders. That would definitely clinch the deal.

Rupert is a problem solver—one of those other coping techniques that I sometimes use. Hey, if you've got a problem, solve it, right? I'll say more about that in the next chapter. But in order to solve a problem, you've got to have at least a little hope that it can be done. You've got to appreciate progress as it comes your way, because that's what keeps you going.

⊞ ⊞ ⊞

When I was about five years old, I wanted to build things. My dad was building a garage at the time, and I watched with fascination as he poured the concrete floor. That was exactly the kind of floor I needed for my fort. I had a brilliant idea—I would make my own concrete! So I grabbed a large tin can that my mom had put in the garbage, filled it with gravel, and then covered the gravel with water. I stirred and stirred. I waited and waited. You know what? Those rocks didn't soften up one bit! Still, I didn't give up. I checked them every day, hoping one day I would see them begin to dissolve into a concrete mush.

This would be what we could call "a lack of progress." It would also be what we refer to as misplaced hope. I was too inexperienced to realize that there was no hope of making concrete through this method, so I kept right on hoping and waiting when I should have been earning pennies to buy a bag of concrete. Hope alone wasn't going to solve my problem. Not this time.

Optimism and hope are important keys to success, but by themselves, they are not enough. We must take positive action and make an intelligent effort to succeed, and then watch for the sparks of progress along the way. If we see no sparks, we must find another way. However, we must believe that there is a way to succeed.

⊞ ⊞ ⊞

For the last 20 years or so, we have had a particular teacher in our school district campaigning for a program for our gifted and talented students. For many years, she alone kept the program alive, even if it was barely breathing, doing whatever she could to provide some kind of enrichment for students who needed the extra intellectual stimulation. She faced obstacles at every turn, with little reason to hope, but with enough of a dream not to give up. Every time another teacher agreed to try a new method, such as grouping or compacting, it was a small victory, and it added another drop of hope into a bucket that seemed impossible to fill. Over the years, her efforts gradually gained momentum. We now have a strong parent support group and additional staff to aid her. Some amazing things have happened. We are always in danger of losing the program, but we are taking steps now, with the help of the administration and faculty, to make it a permanent part of our curriculum.

This teacher who has kept things going for all these years is soon to retire. She never thought she'd see this day, and yet she had some rabbits she couldn't let go of. She saw the sparks in the tunnel and knew there was light. It still existed. She just had to keep going.

⊞　⊞　⊞

My mother has a friend named Petunia. Petunia is gifted. She has gifted children. Gifted children have been known, here and there, to struggle with finding an appropriate educational environment. Thanks to Petunia's experience with her son Eugene, I have hope that I will be able to help my children find the right educational "fit."

Eugene is a middle child. When he was three years old, his quirks were overwhelming. He had several self-imposed dressing restrictions and a collection of costumes. His brain and body both ran on such high speed that his mother couldn't keep up with him. She worked all day to keep him entertained, but when his little brother was born, she decided that she either had to send Eugene to preschool for two mornings a week or rent a padded cell.

So Petunia searched for a suitable preschool. She met a lovely woman who was a mother with a teaching degree who held a preschool in her home. This woman's philosophy was total freedom of expression. She didn't mind that Eugene showed up in his cowboy costume, and she didn't mind that Eugene loved to paint. She didn't even care if he restricted the paint to the paper provided for him or if he preferred to paint the fence or the little girl standing next to him. After about two weeks of Eugene painting anything or anybody he wanted, his mother decided it was time to look for another school.

Her next stop was a city parks and recreation school. It seemed to be a nice little class that met in a large gym with loving teachers and lots of stimulating toys. Eugene would have room to run and plenty of opportunity to be busy—hopefully busy within a few boundaries, yes, but busy. However, every day when Petunia picked Eugene up from school, she found all of the children sitting on the floor enjoying a story while they waited for their parents—all but Eugene. He waited at the doorway, eager to go home.

Petunia tried one more time. She found a nearby school run by a local church. It had an opening, and so she made an appointment to visit the school with Eugene. When they arrived, the director gave them a brief tour of the play yard and the classrooms. Eugene looked up at Petunia and said, "This is the school."

She leaned over to him and asked, "What do you mean, 'This is *the* school'?"

Eugene said, "Well, this school has carpet, and I always wear shorts. The last school had floors that were too cold, and I couldn't sit down."

So what had seemed like anxiety at the last school was anxiety, but it wasn't about what was happening at the school. It was the floor.

Eugene loved the third school. Each day he went to school and learned something that opened up his world a little wider. In the beginning, this worried him. He wasn't used to learning new things at school. On his first day, he learned how to tie his shoes. Petunia said, "That's wonderful!"

He asked, "Can I still go back?"

Eugene was aware that preschool had certain expectations of him. He didn't want to meet those expectations too quickly, because he thought he would have to graduate and wouldn't be able to return.

But about two weeks into his school attendance, Petunia arrived to find out that Eugene was in the director's office. "Oh great," she thought. "What has he done?"

As she walked to the office, she told herself that surely there were still other schools to explore. They could move on. When she arrived at the office, she found her son in the midst of a work project. Eugene was happily filing folders in alphabetical order for the director. He had found a fit!

Not only did he remain at that school, but Petunia eventually went back to school herself to earn a teaching degree, and then she taught at that same school for 17 years. Apparently, it was a good fit for both of them. It's a good thing she didn't give up before she found it.

We never know when we are just one step away from discovery. We've got to be like the guys in the long white coats in the laboratories who keep working away, trying this, trying that, and trying the space in between this and that, always looking, hoping for an answer, hoping that even if the next experiment doesn't solve the problem, it will at least bring them a step closer to the solution. Maybe the situation is overwhelming, or maybe we'll find a puzzle piece that suddenly enlightens us and connects all of the seemingly chaotic pieces and organizes them into a sensible mess.

Just like my parents in the flood, while it is important to be aware of the problems, and to make every attempt to resolve them, we must also be aware that there is still a sun shining behind the clouds. At some point, the rain really will stop, even if the end is not yet in sight.

Although giftedness complicates everything, whether it's education, work, or relationships, on the bright side, well, on the bright side...read on.

2: Another Way Around It

I believe that some labels are good for kids—they broaden rather than confine. I've labeled Rupert as a problem solver. He likes that label. I do, too.

When he gets really frustrated because things aren't going his way, I tell him, "It's okay. You'll figure it out. You're a problem solver." I catch a look on his face that says, "Oh yeah, that's right. I am. I almost forgot."

Sometimes he'll be just plain grumpy, and I'll send him to his room to pull himself together. If I remember to send him in with the problem-solving reminder, he'll still go in crying, but after he lies on his bed for a few minutes, he'll get quiet. Five minutes later, he'll come out of his room with a solution.

One of Rupert's coping skills is finding another way around something. He has a long history of creative solutions to ordinary problems. When he was only three, he wanted to make a necklace, and he needed some string. Since I wasn't home at the time to get him some, he attempted to solve the problem himself. I found his solution the next day when I went to make a phone call, but I couldn't get a dial tone. I looked down at the phone and realized that somebody had cut off the cord. Great. But Rupert had solved *his* problem.

So I commended Rupert on his problem-solving efforts and then had a little discussion about destroying other people's property and, oh yes, the dangers of electricity.

Rupert has always been extra sensitive to noise. Since his older brothers Otto and Stanley both played in the school bands for years, we often attended band concerts, and the concerts were always loud. I spent every concert out in the hallway listening to muffled music, because Rupert wouldn't allow me to get any closer. He would sit in my arms with his hands over his ears, crying if he was too close to the sound.

When he was about four, Rupert surprised us one evening when he agreed to go to the concert without any tears or complaints. When my children surprise me with compliant behavior, I have learned to be grateful and not question the change, though in the back of my head, a little voice always tells me to investigate the matter further, because—in spite of my best efforts—compliant behavior is not the norm for my children.

Rupert wanted to bring a "toy" with him, and I didn't argue. It was a nice, soft, insulated lunch bag, and I couldn't see any harm in it. He put things inside of it. He took them out. Just like with the black knit snow hat, Rupert's imagination can keep him busy with simple objects for hours.

The lunch bag kept him busy for about 15 minutes. The moment the concert began, he stopped playing with the bag and pulled it over his head and sat there, content to listen to the music through a layer of vinyl-sandwiched padding, and he stayed that way for most of the concert. He was prepared. He had solved the problem.

I just kept my fingers crossed hoping that he could still breathe and that he would value oxygen over sensitive ears if he had to make a judgment call.

⠿ ⠿ ⠿

Recently, Rupert began developing his own sign language. He made a chart that showed each word with an accompanied diagram of exactly how the hands and fingers should be held, and for some signals, arrows that showed movement. In this case, he was solving a problem that already had a perfectly good solution, but he wanted to find his *own* solution.

Creative brains often solve problems in an unconventional manner. Sometimes this is good. It can lead to amazing new discoveries and technological advances. Sometimes it's not so good. Sometimes the challenge and the adventure become a game in themselves.

When my niece Fritzie was four, she turned doorknobs by standing on her head and using her feet. She had two perfectly capable hands that would have done the job more quickly and efficiently, but hey, where was the fun in that?

This sort of ingenuity isn't unique to four-year-olds. My son Otto and his college friends decided one day that there had to be another, possibly far more interesting, way to drink out of the drinking fountain. They tried hoisting themselves above the drinking fountain so they could drink upside down while standing on their hands. Not real smart, but pretty creative. They met with some success, except for the boy who inhaled more water through his nose than he drank with his mouth. They did take some thought to support the drinking fountain and their added weight by piling textbooks on a chair and wedging it under the metal fountain. Textbooks have to be good for something, right? Fortunately, the fountain held up, or they might have found themselves in a more serious position that required even greater problem-solving skills—like how to pay a repair bill or how to avoid suspension.

Sometimes creative brains just need a little exercise. They look for a new way around a problem simply because they are bored with the more conventional approach. This does not always lead to breakthroughs in the way we do things. Sometimes it's only for fun. And sometimes, as in the case with the drinking fountain, the old ways really do turn out to be the best.

※　※　※

There are other times when a person has the creative ability to think around the problem, yet doesn't have complete enough knowledge to *understand* the problem. Details are important. Sometimes we expect rapid learners to be terrific problem solvers, and then we don't know why they're not getting it. The crux of the problem is often that they don't have enough information to work with. Sometimes we assume that "gifted" means "all-knowing," and that's unfair. Just because a brain has an amazing ability to grasp knowledge when it's presented to it doesn't mean that the brain can pull solutions out of thin air, never having been exposed to that information before.

When my oldest son Stanley was six, he asked me if he was part Mexican. Because I didn't want to go into fractions at the time, instead of telling him that he was one-eighth Mexican, I told him he was just a little Mexican. The next day, he handed me a self-portrait of himself, pen on paper, and the page was empty except for a little tiny, sombrero-wearing stick figure at the bottom. He said, "See, Mom? I'm a little Mexican!"

In his six-year-old experience, "little" did not mean "partial"; it meant "small."

At that same age, when Stanley found out that I was attending a baby shower and that several of my friends would be present, he asked, "So how big is the tub anyway? About this big?" and he stretched out his arms as far as he could reach on either side. In his mind, a shower was a thing you stood in and got really wet and soapy.

Never mind that Stanley had taught himself to read by the time he was two-and-a-half years old. A fast brain can only operate on the information it has to work with.

🀫 🀫 🀫

When Otto was about five, I remember he used to play cops and robbers with his friends. The moment he had the bad guy in his sight, he would point an imaginary gun at the perpetrator and yell, "Freeze! You're undressed!" He knew what it was to be undressed, and even though I can't imagine what was going through his mind and why he thought a policeman would yell that to a criminal, it sure made a heck of a lot more sense than yelling, "You're under arrest!" because after all, what did "arrest" mean? To him, it wasn't even a real word.

Speaking of words, gifted kids often solve problems by making up their own words to express concepts that they can't put a name on. To Rupert, tree stumps were once "wood signs" because they represented a place where wood had been. Pandora called Twinkies "tweeny pinkies," because the word "Twinkies" had no context in her mind. She used the word "salty" to describe a twinkling sound, because that was the best word she knew of to describe what she was hearing. She had the concept but not the word.

This sort of thing can go the other way as well. Sometimes the kids have the words but not the concepts. When Stanley was about four, he used to sit next to my husband and quietly read over his shoulder. College texts on business are probably not interesting to most four-year-olds. Stanley was only partially interested. He could easily read and enjoy pronouncing the words, but of course he didn't comprehend the true meaning of "compounding interest."

Rupert struggled with the concept of "tomorrow" for more than a year. He couldn't picture it. He couldn't grasp it, because it was eternally elusive. Tomorrow was always the next day, but it was never here. Even with the help of a calendar as a visual aid, he just didn't get it. He takes things literally. When he came home from kindergarten, he boasted that he never went to the bathroom at school. I told him that he definitely ought to, should he ever feel the need, and I asked him why he didn't. He said, "It costs money."

This was news to me, so I asked his teacher about it. After a few moments of confusion, the explanation dawned on her, and she laughed. "Sometimes the kids need to use the bathroom a little too often, and so when they raise their hand, I say, 'Okay, but it'll cost you.' I had no idea they were taking me literally."

Since Rupert was unfamiliar with that common slang expression, he figured, hey, no potty time without some loose change to the teacher.

When we took a family vacation, we found some souvenirs in different languages. Pandora has always had a fascination for France, so she chose a French inscription. I helped Rupert, who was then about five, pick out a souvenir in English. I assured him that it was the right language for him.

"What is it?" he asked.

"English."

He was upset and disappointed with me that I would try to fool him like that. "*English?*" Then he said, "I wanted *Human!*"

Even the older kids face confusion with words sometimes. Magnolia was at a friend's house one night when her friend's family ordered pizza—with artichoke hearts. Magnolia was horrified. In her mind, she confused artichokes with anchovies—all those "A" foods sound so much alike that you can hardly blame her, especially when she's never laid eyes on them before. Since she really wasn't in the mood for little fish hearts on pizza, she declined. Fortunately, she mentioned this to her friend, who, after the laughter subsided, explained the difference. All was well. She had a fine dinner, which included vegetables.

With all of the innocence of youth and the lack of worldly experience, imagine what a child thinks of when he hears the term "serial killer" on the news. After all, why would anyone want to kill a bowl of cereal? How is it done, anyway? And you can be arrested for that? Really?

▦ ▦ ▦

Young children are the obvious examples of inexperience, but age does not always bring every person the same set of experiences, and it is still possible to mistake giftedness or advanced learning for all-knowingness or good judgment. They aren't the same.

When Magnolia was 13, I decided to take advantage of my husband's out-of-town trip to redecorate the basement. We were going to pull a "While You Were Out," and I needed help from all my kids, because we have a rather large basement, and it needed a lot of work. I set myself up to paint the family room ceiling and walls, and I gave Magnolia what I thought was the much simpler and quicker task of painting the basement bathroom ceiling and walls. We were both armed with the same tools—a can of paint and a brush. While I painted away, I kept talking to Magnolia through the partially closed bathroom door to ask her if she was doing all right. She was frustrated, but she said yeah, it was going all right. I kept painting, wondering when she might emerge saying she had finished. This went on for nearly two hours, until I had the family room almost finished. Finally, exasperated with her slower rate of progress, I climbed off my stepladder and went into the bathroom to check on her. There she stood in the middle of the floor, reaching up with the paintbrush toward the ceiling. I'm surprised that I was able to see her at all, as she was wearing layers of camouflaging drips of cream-colored paint, which blended nicely into the layers of drips of paint on the floor, on the cabinets and countertops, on the mirror, and on the toilet seat. Lovely.

"What are you doing? How did you get so much paint everywhere?"

"I'm *trying*," she growled.

"Show me what you're doing."

So she sloshed the brush in the bucket, loaded it with a cup-and-a-half of paint, and splatted it on the ceiling above her while most of the paint dripped down in streams onto her arm and head.

"Uh, Magnolia, can I see that brush for a minute?"

"Gladly."

I took the slimy, paint-covered brush and showed her how to dip just the tip of it in the can, tap off the excess, and then brush it on to the ceiling without a drip.

25

She glared at me. That icy teenage glare. "Gee, thanks for showing me how *now*."

My mistake. I had assumed too much: one, that Magnolia would think to paint properly, never having done it before, and two, that she would have an interest in learning how.

In this case, not only did her inexperience get in her way of problem solving, but her lack of desire to do the job well rather than quickly also got in her way. I should have known. This was the same girl who, at age nine, washed my kitchen floor by pouring water from the bucket onto the floor and then using towels to sop it up—before she swept.

🞝 🞝 🞝

Sometimes creative problem solvers let their creativity run amok, unhindered by warning alarms triggered by either reason or experience. Like Rupert's phone-cord filching, a little reason and experience can go a long way to soften the consequences of unbridled creativity.

When my seven-year-old cousin was asked to clean out his aquarium, he carefully took out each goldfish, scrubbed it with soap and water, and then popped it in the microwave to dry. He didn't let common sense (which is somewhat less common when you're seven years old, even if you *are* very bright) and logic interfere with his goal of providing a clean environment for his fish. After all, *he* took a bath with soap and water, and it didn't hurt *him*, and how could he possibly have known the danger of microwaves? He just knew they worked quickly, and by Jove, he needed to get those fish back in their tank as soon as possible. No doubt those goldfish were anxious to get back in there even sooner, like before they died. Somehow, he missed the whole "why dry them off only to put them in water again" angle. His intent was to do his job thoroughly.

Being gifted may mean that you have exceptional prob-lem-solving skills, but it doesn't mean you know everything. I'm pretty creative and have some good problem-solving skills, but

I'm not about to do anything with electricity in my house that requires repair or rewiring. I know that my inexperience and lack of knowledge could have disastrous results. I might be able to figure out the most efficient way to run the wires, or at least make a really cool design with them, but there's a pretty good chance I'd come out with a few jolting experiences and potentially even a house fire. Not a good idea.

We could write off the goldfish bath example simply as inexperienced youth, but it also reflects only too well my brother-in-law's problem-solving style. He's an exceptionally bright man with so much enthusiasm for coming up with ingenious solutions that he doesn't let his brain get in the way of his creative impulses. Think Tim "The Tool Man" Taylor. When the shower curtain fails to keep the water from flooding the bathroom floor, probably the best and easiest solution is to find out who isn't tucking the curtain in properly and teach them the finer arts of curtain tucking. Instead, my brother-in-law found a long, rectangular flower planter and nailed it to the bottom of the shower to catch the water. Smart man. But in this case, not such great problem-solving skills. A brain can be moving at the speed of light and still miss the mark.

Looking at the bright side, my sister has some great stories to tell. And now that he has a little more experience, I'll bet that next time, he'll try a different solution—if his wife lets him anywhere near a toolbox again.

❖ ❖ ❖

Some creative solutions are unconventional but harmless, and they do the job fairly well. When my uncle gets a spot on his shirt, he just turns it inside out. He's not at all averse to wearing a woman's shirt if his are all in the laundry. He doesn't care. The point is that he's wearing a shirt. This is the same guy who once tied a helium balloon to his glasses to keep them from rubbing on his nose.

When my youngest sister Hortense was five, she got dressed for church one morning, and she looked like an almost perfectly normal little girl until we looked more closely. When she couldn't find any tights to wear under her dress, she improvised with a woman's girdle and a mismatched pair of white knee socks. The socks were pulled up over the bottom of the girdle and, at first glance, looked like a wrinkly pair of tights. We discovered her fashion faux pas only *after* we were already at church. It was okay, though. Hortense was in good company. We also discovered that my other sister, seven-year-old Edna, had rolled up her flannel pajama bottoms under her dress, which fluffed her skirt out nicely. If you add my mom's attempts at home-sewn garments and haphazard hairdos, oh yes, we were a sharp-looking family back then. Definitely unconventional.

When Otto was in high school, he didn't care much about fashion. I tried to buy him a new pair of shoes because I was embarrassed by his old ones, but he said he didn't need new shoes. If the bottom of his shoe came unglued, why, he'd just duct tape it right back on. I guess he thought he was saving their soles. (Couldn't resist. Sorry.) Eventually, those shoes developed such a thick shell of duct tape that he could pull the shoe out and just wear the duct tape. He finally decided to turn them into boots so he could tuck his jeans into them. They were very attractive.

🏮 🏮 🏮

Some creative solutions are harmless but effective, even if they aren't efficient. Sometimes the joy lies in the challenge rather than the solution.

When my brother Myron was in high school, he had great difficulty waking up on time in the mornings. He would set his alarm clock at night and then smack the off button every morning while he was still in a half-conscious state. He reasoned that if he moved his alarm clock farther away, he would have to wake up in order to get to it. It worked. The only problem was that when he was woozy, his body told his brain that it didn't want to wake up, and it didn't want to go over to the alarm to turn it off. Was there a compromise? Myron's brain went to work and devised a mechanical way to reach the alarm clock without getting up and without moving the clock closer. He rounded up odds and ends from his room and arranged them in a way that would create a chain reaction that would end with a smack on the snooze button.

He was now sleeping in past the alarm again. He moved the clock even farther way, woke up on time for a few days, and then devised still another way to reach the clock (using mechanical aids) without getting up. This process continued until Myron had a contraption going halfway around his room with his alarm clock at the far end of it. Ultimately, I don't remember if he ever learned to get up or not, but he did spend some great problem-solving time learning basic mechanical skills and principles.

⊞ ⊞ ⊞

When my mom's friend Petunia moved to Hawaii, she discovered that it was hot, and she decided to solve the problem by lopping off her hair. She soon realized that a short hairdo just wasn't her style. No, instead she wanted "perky hair like Sandra Dee." The problem was that her hair was too short, and instead of blonde, it was gray. Or rather, it was white on top, gray in the middle, with a darker hue underneath. When my mother suggested that Petunia dye her hair to even out the color, Petunia refused. She wanted to age gracefully. Apparently looking perky like Sandra Dee had something to do with aging gracefully.

Petunia decided to order a hairpiece—a fluffy ponytail—to wear until her own hair grew out again. She ordered one, and a month later the box arrived. The moment she opened the box, she knew she was in trouble. The hairpiece was a salt and pepper color, but heavy on the pepper. She boxed it back up and requested a different shade. So far, other than wanting to look like Sandra Dee, Petunia seems like a normal, logical, reasonable human being, right? But she's not. No, she's actually a creative problem solver.

Her first impression of the second hairpiece was that it resembled a rat. Rats are not perky. Rats do not remind anyone of Sandra Dee. No good. So she returned the rat and tried one more time. The third hairpiece was too white. By this time she had had enough. She was not about to return the thing. No, she would just make it work. So she wore it, hoping that somehow it would darken with time. Every day she looked at that hairpiece, determined to make it work, to make it darker, to make it just the right shade. No matter how much energy she spent on thinking the hairpiece into a darker shade, her mental powers failed to do the trick.

One day an idea came to her. She decided to experiment with cornstarch to take off the shine, and then pepper to darken it up. After treating it with several other condiments, the thing looked like Barbie doll hair that a dog had dragged around and slept on for nine weeks. Petunia was getting desperate when she asked Myrna for her advice. They read the tag on the hairpiece, which had heretofore gone unnoticed, and the tag said, "No hairspray, and *never* use a blow dryer." It didn't say, "No condiments."

It occurs to me as I write this that warning labels are inadequate for the fast brain. I mean, surely, if a manufacturer feels it necessary to warn its customers that rat poison is for external use only or that coffee is hot, then it only stands to reason that a hairpiece should come with a cautionary warning about condiments.

Well, Petunia and Myrna remained undaunted. This "rat" could be rehabilitated and refined. They set to work washing and combing, and Myrna the Artist got out her watercolors. She mixed until she had the perfect shade to match Petunia's tri-toned hair. She squeezed the hairpiece in a color wash and then, yes, did the unthinkable. She got out a blow dryer and blasted the rat into submission.

It was perfect. Petunia loved it. She felt like Sandra Dee—just as long as she didn't wear her hairpiece out in the rain.

Perhaps it would have been wise to waterproof it with a slick coat of polyurethane.

⊞   ⊞   ⊞

Just remember, no matter how many problems we solve, there are always more waiting for us in the wings. How cool is that? Always new challenges, right?

Yay.

Gifted problem solvers need good information, experience, and the proper tools to help them solve problems. Even McGuyver, the famous TV problem solver, couldn't have solved all of those problems if his script writers hadn't written in plenty of knowledge and experience in his past for him to draw upon. And if he could stop a criminal with nothing more than a lightbulb and a peanut butter sandwich, he was still relying on tools, albeit unconventional ones.

When I think of McGuyver, I think of one of my nieces. I'll call her Denise, get it? De Niece?

When Denise was 18 months old, there was an occasion when she desperately wanted to climb up in a chair, but she wasn't tall enough or strong enough to get up there herself. Her older sister, three-year-old Olive, decided to help Denise achieve her goal. Olive wasn't a whole lot stronger than Denise, but she tried to grab Denise's legs and give her a boost. It was no use. Olive just fell to the floor on her stomach. Denise took a moment to assess the situation, then stepped on Olive's back and climbed up onto the chair. Easy. She used her knowledge, experience, and most importantly, the tools that were at hand to solve the problem.

Okay, so maybe the rest of us avoid stepping on someone else to get where we want to go. Apparently, sweet, innocent, 18-month-old babies are unaware of scruples like that. After all, Olive wanted to help, and ultimately, that's what she did, right?

⊞   ⊞   ⊞

You know, it's interesting. Some people wait for the paper every morning so they can do the daily crossword puzzle. Others can't stand the wait, or if they prefer to do more than one puzzle in one sitting, they go out and buy themselves a book of crosswords or sudokus or cryptograms. I recently purchased a couple of different books of brainteasers, because I knew my kids would love them. As for me, I began doing sudokus a few years ago when I first found them in our local paper. Eventually, I looked up a sudoku website online and began attempting the more challenging puzzles, with the added challenge of trying to beat my own best time. I began to spend way too much time online attempting to outdo myself. I finally had to quit cold turkey, because my sudoku habit was out of control. However, I did feel better when I saw another lady at Otto's high school graduation who, instead of listening to the valedictorian, had a pencil and a book of sudokus. At least I was able to quell my addiction long enough to sit through the graduation ceremony.

Our brains long for challenges. We're willing to invest time and money for opportunities to solve artificial problems when there is no reward other than the feeling of success that comes when we rise to a challenge and overcome it. Now if we could only transfer that attitude to the real world, where there are many problems yet unsolved. Problems are a dime a dozen, and solutions promise more than the mere satisfaction of a job done well.

If we can see a problem coming and think, "Hey, this one will be a challenge, and I *love* challenges!" we will be set up in a better frame of mind to tackle the problem head on, rather than being intimidated by it.

Problems are going to arise on every side, but it's okay. Creative fast-brain people are problem solvers. It's a good label to have.

3: Too Much Information— Or Not Enough

Otto suggested that this chapter should be all about girls, because after a somewhat frustrating year of dating at college, he says they either give him too much information or not enough. Relationships are tricky places to hang out, because communication requires a balance. No matter what our gender, we may not agree on what information is the most pertinent to the relationship. Or we may assume that other people already know things about us when they simply don't. Sometimes we assume too much.

When my sister Darleen got married, she couldn't wait for her first Christmas together with her husband. After all, Christmas at our house had always been a big deal, and she wanted to reproduce that wonderful experience in her own home. She set up the Christmas tree, decorated it, and began piling gifts for her new hubby under the branches. It seemed like every other day, she added something new. She waited with great anticipation for Christmas morning. She *did* think it somewhat curious that her hubby didn't have anything under the tree for her, but she wrote it off as him being secretive, with maybe something special hidden away until the last moment. On Christmas morning, Darleen woke up to a huge pile of presents—for her husband. There was nothing under the tree for her. Nothing hidden or secretive, either.

I know this sounds difficult to believe, but her new hubby was simply unaware of the expectations she had for the two of them for Christmas gift giving. Sure, he saw the presents piling up under the tree, but he didn't think much about it. When he was growing up, his family did things differently. He is a very intelligent man, but he does not always pick up well on clues. His mind was busy somewhere else.

Fortunately, their marriage *did* survive the disaster. He learned, very quickly, that Darleen had different expectations than he did when it came to holidays, and she came to realize that her hubby, though often clueless, was certainly not loveless. He just needed a few really obvious verbal clues and reminders. Of course, it didn't hurt that he later bought her a baby grand for a Christmas gift, just to redeem himself.

〓〓 〓〓 〓〓

Sometimes gifted people pick up information at an exceptionally quick pace. Other times, when their brains are someplace else, in a galaxy far, far away, the information doesn't even get a chance to sink through the scalp.

A few years ago, when Otto was a freshly-turned 12-year-old, we took a road trip with my sister Gertrude and her family. We traveled from Montana through Idaho, Oregon, and then down the coast through the redwoods of California. We stopped at a place with huge statues of Paul Bunyan and Babe the Blue Ox. Paul was tall enough that the best the kids could do was climb onto the toe of his giant boot. Babe the Blue Ox was large enough that an adult could easily walk beneath his underbelly.

Fifteen-year-old Stanley's first comment, which Otto apparently didn't hear or pay attention to, was, "Hey look! The ox is anatomically correct!"

Stanley went on and on about it while Otto joined the other kids in attempting to scale Paul's boot. Stanley wanted to get a picture of the, ahem, "scenery," because 15-year-old boys are weird like that. My hubby told him, "Don't take any pictures without people in them!"

So Stanley asked Otto to stand under the ox, which Otto was glad to do, as he was in a good mood and didn't mind being in a photo or two. But Otto was determined that he could only be bossed around so much, and if he was going to be in the photo, he was going to do it his way. He stood directly beneath Babe and extended his hands above his head and placed them on the only part of the statue that he could reach. His brain was focused on being photographed; it didn't stop to evaluate exactly what pieces made up the underside of the giant ox.

Stanley yelled, "Otto, don't do that! Sit down!"

Stubborn and clueless, Otto yelled back, "No!" and he smiled for the picture.

By this time, Gertrude, her husband Ignatius, and my hubby and I were laughing so hard that we had tears streaming down our faces and we could hardly breathe. I think we all felt some sort of obligation to help Otto out by informing him of his, uh, situation, but none of us could stop laughing enough to get a word out.

In the meantime, Stanley tried to convince Otto to please, *please* sit down. Still, Otto persisted in maintaining his current position. So Stanley snapped, and a highly embarrassing photo was made.

As we adults pulled ourselves together enough to herd the kids back into our vehicles, Otto noticed that we couldn't quit giggling, but he didn't give it a second thought. It wasn't until we were belted in and on our way down the road that we finally managed to get our speaking voices back, and Hubby and I explained to Otto exactly why Stanley wanted him to sit down and why it might be wise to listen to his brother next time, just in case. Awareness is sometimes a slippery thing.

⊞ ⊞ ⊞

Information is another. These kids soak it in no matter where they find it. You can't keep it from them. Our second grader, Rupert, is always one to pick up on information, even if he doesn't have a place to file it in his brain yet. For a long time, he would say his prayers and ask for "the sick to be reflicted." We didn't correct him, because it was so darn cute and he was so darn sincere. He likes new words. A few weeks ago, his teacher told him what the word "regret" means. It's been one of his favorite words ever since, and he uses it every chance he gets. He likes to use phrases that he hears other people use, like "just my style" or "in the middle of nowhere." He told me that he decided to build his ninja castle "in the middle of nowhere," because that was the only place that would have enough room to hold it.

But just when I think I'm dealing with an innocent and clueless child, Rupert demonstrates a surprising capacity for gathering and processing information.

We tried a satellite dish for one year, at which time Magnolia and Otto both said, "This is pointless. We just watch the same things over and over again." With a response like that from two teenagers, we couldn't justify continuing the monthly expense of lulling our children into a semi-vegetative state for a few hours every night, when even *they* recognized that their brain cells were dying a slow and painful death.

However, Pandora and Rupert disagreed. They didn't mind losing a few brain cells. They could always grow more. And in fact, four-year-old Rupert's brain cells were getting a pretty good workout. The minute that anything on TV came on, he was there, sucking in every image, every word, every cool new phrase that he didn't understand but wanted to use anyway.

I realized that if the TV stayed on, Rupert would forget his much-loved Legos and Lincoln Logs and become one with the glass screen, so I thought, "Hmm, maybe if I switch it to something boring, like the news, I can still watch and figure out what's going on in the world, he'll have background noise, and he'll still play with his Legos."

Ri-i-i-ight.

The minute the TV was turned on, Rupert dropped everything and perched himself on the couch. When his dad walked into the room, Rupert ran up to him. "Hey, Dad, guess what, there's this plane, and its wheels won't come down, and it's flying in circles over the ocean until it can land, and there are people on board…." He went on and on in one long, breathless, run-on sentence about every detail he'd just heard and seen on the news.

So then I figured we had to be more careful about the news. I really didn't want Rupert repeating every detail of a violent crime to anyone, and I didn't want him replaying it in his own little mind. So if he *had* to have the TV on, I tuned to infomercials. I hoped they would bore him silly. But no. Rupert watched while I tried to get my work done.

He would run over to me and say, "Mom, you should get a SuperStep Stepladder. It folds in half, and it turns into two ladders, and you can get to all of those hard-to-reach places!" or, "Mom, hey, guess what? If you buy this Hot-in-a-Flash Cooker, it will cook the chicken all the way through while you watch!" or, "Hey, hey, we should get a home mortgage loan. It'll save you money, Mom!"

That's when the TV went off for good. You know, I've never been one to inundate my children with educational materials. Some, yes, but a constant flow, no. I figure that they need to be kids and dream of ninjas and dragons and fairy tale characters, and when I see what the little brains are taking in, I realize that I had better offer them something a little more nutritious than mental junk food. They're living in the middle of this stuff, after all.

❖ ❖ ❖

I recently purchased some DVDs of college courses on tape called "The Great Courses from the Teaching Company." I started out thinking, "I'll order that one, and maybe that one," and then I went nuts and ordered a bunch more. I bought them for myself, but I also had my kids in mind. If I had the DVDs on and my kids happened to walk in the room, they just might learn a little something. Sure enough, after one session, which was an introduction to physics, Rupert and Pandora were all aglow about black holes and time traveling and tunneling. Pandora, especially, just eats it up. She went to school and told her teacher about force and acceleration and mass and how they affect each other. She thinks she might want to be a physicist some day.

My nephew Roland is another one who can't get enough information. He looks for it everywhere. He has all of the calories and nutritional information memorized from fast food menus, and he orders accordingly. "Nope, can't get that sandwich—too many calories." He'll work for his information, too. The morning after the last day of school, his mom Hortense woke up to find him sitting on the couch with a pad of paper and a pencil. He was trying to figure out exactly how many days, hours, and minutes he had spent in school, and he was temporarily stuck as he tried to remember how many early outs and holidays they'd had that year. Why is this information important to him? I can't imagine, but his brain apparently wants to know this stuff.

Information is important to hungry minds. They can't function efficiently without the right information, no matter how gifted they are. And you never know when a little healthy information will be just what the doctor ordered to grease the gears.

⊞　⊞　⊞

Then sometimes, too much information clogs the gears, or at least it happens at times to my gears. One day when Otto came home from high school, I asked him how his day was, and he told me about his calculus class. "Mom, I was doing this problem: You have one function and you are supposed to find out when it is decreasing and when it is concave up, and everybody thought you were supposed to find out when it was doing both at the same time, but you were really supposed to find out when it was concave up, when it was decreasing, and when it was both."

At that point, my brain went into a paralytic stupor stage. It was temporarily out of order. I didn't speak Otto's language—I needed a translator.

I have found myself lost in communication issues on other occasions as well. I don't always speak the language of the person who is trying to communicate with me. If I am listening to a lecture on a subject that interests me and that I have some experience with, at least enough to give the subject some context, then I'm fine. I comprehend, and the information finds a home in my gray matter. However, I can't mentally catalog sequential information fast enough to make sense of it, especially if it is given as a rapid series of factual information soundbites—not even if the list is short. There are some things I must take the time to translate.

A friend tried to give me directions to get to his house. Now I admit that I am direction-impaired to start with. Whether we're talking a cardinal direction or a simple left and right, I have to think about it. Some people remind themselves by forming an L with their left thumb and forefinger with palm facing away from them. However, as my sister Darleen said, as she tried this approach with both hands to find the L, "Left? Left? Which one is left?" Because, like me, she suddenly can't remember which way an L is supposed to face.

My friend said, "Karen, just take a right off the freeway, turn left on 1600 North, and then turn right on Heppleworth. I'm the second house on the right."

I stood there in a stupor. Rights and lefts had come flying at my brain so quickly that I hadn't had time to sort them out. Fortunately, my friend was quick to recognize my confusion and understood that he needed to communicate with me in a different language.

This time, he used his body as he spoke. "Karen, take a right off the freeway," he twisted his body rightward, "turn left on 1600 North" he twisted his body leftward, "and turn right on

Heppleworth Street," and he turned rightward again. Then he said very slowly, "I am the second house on the right."

Finally it all made sense to me. Even though that happened almost 20 years ago, I will never forget those directions, because I could *see* them. I can still see them. Some people digest information best by hearing it, while others, like me, need to see it. Even when we all have access to the same information, we will each retain different aspects of that information, depending on our preferred learning style, our individual experiences that relate to that information, and our ability to process that information at different rates of speed.

It's great to have the information you need, but when it comes to your brain out of turn, before the foundation has been laid for you to comprehend that information, it's like Rupert and his concept of "the middle of nowhere" or "the sick to be reflicted." Or like me with directions. You have no place to put the information. You get lost, and sometimes you don't even realize it. When I'm talking to people like Otto and the topic is something like physics, I realize it.

Personally, I don't enjoy being lost. I'd much rather feel the firmness of a foundation of a healthy knowledge base beneath my feet. I feel much more comfortable when I'm equipped with the information I need to comprehend the situations that arise around me.

⊞　⊞　⊞

Information can be helpful when you least expect it. My dad Harold used to dress up in a Santa suit every year, and our family would go Christmas caroling and bring plates of cookies to friends' houses. One year, Harold went to a home where a young boy said, "You're not the real Santa!"

Harold immediately responded, "How do you know I'm not?"

"Prove it that you are. What's the capital of Nebraska?"

"Lincoln."

The boy was taken back. "Okay then, what's the capital of Florida?"

"Tallahassee."

"Hey, you *are* the real Santa!"

Now Harold is not one to keep up on his state capitals. He'd much rather spend his time with his nose to a machine, learning the secrets of its inner workings. However, my youngest sister Hortense had just taken a test on the states and their capitals, and lucky for Santa Harold, he had helped her study the capitals.

🏮 🏮 🏮

This year, in her first real job, Magnolia works as a cashier at a fast food restaurant. Recently, a man approached her and said, "Habla Español?"

She answered as best she could, "A little." She had, after all, taken an entire year of Spanish as a freshman. She is technically fluent under specific circumstances, such as asking where the ladies' room is or saying, "How are you? My name is Magnolia." ¿Como esta? Se llama Magnolia.

So the man proceeded to give her his order in Spanish, while Magnolia sweated bullets trying to decipher his words. She heard "no queso" and knew that "queso" meant "cheese," but the rest of the order required her best guesses at translation based on her limited experience. At the end of his order, she used hand motions to ask him if the order was "for here or to go." He gave her an answer she couldn't understand, so she smiled and said, "Okay," and pressed the "to go" button.

A couple of minutes later, when he picked up his order, he said to Magnolia in perfect English, "Thank you. I enjoy speaking Spanish, but I rarely have the opportunity."

I think Magnolia may have muttered a few things under her breath, and probably not in Spanish, either. The good news is that after the man finished his meal, which wasn't "to go" after all, he asked for the manager and told him what an excellent job Magnolia was doing.

State capitals, "queso,"—every little bit of information helps. You never know what piece of information will come in handy. Most information, as long as it is appropriate for the emotional maturity of a child, and as long as it isn't manipulative, like the infomercials, becomes more valuable once it is given a context. Information is one of the most valuable problem-solving tools and coping tools that any brain can put away in its toolbox.

⊞   ⊞   ⊞

Sometimes access to information leads to embarrassing or uncomfortable situations. I have to remind myself that I am educating my child for the sake of my child, not for my own social comfort. I can readily admit when my children are talking over my head. Unfortunately, not all embarrassments are so easily brushed off.

For example, last summer, when he was just six, I took Rupert to one of those big warehouse stores where everything is sold in bulk. I was on a shopping spree, and it is our habit to stock up on things, especially if they are on sale. With five children, you go through a lot of groceries. Heck, with Otto alone, we go through a lot of groceries. On this particular day, I had a little extra food money budgeted, and so I was doing an extensive amount of grocery shopping, even for me. I grabbed the largest cart I could find, which was pretty much the back of a flatbed truck only on much smaller wheels, and I tried to maneuver my way through the store, hoping that the other shoppers would just write me off as someone who was restocking a restaurant or two. Driving is not my best skill. And just because my grocery vehicle isn't motorized, it doesn't mean it is any less dangerous. So I was already calling attention to myself with my clumsiness, but I'm used to that. I just apologize a lot.

But Rupert was on an end-of-the-world kick, which is one of his favorites, because he is fascinated by hot lava and earthquakes and tornadoes. So while he was talking about what we would do in case the end of the world came, I was stacking piles and piles of food on my cart and feeling embarrassed. Yes, all I needed was a sandwich board saying, "The end of the world is tomorrow!" I don't know if people were making wide circles around me as they passed because of my driving or because they thought I might hand them pamphlets about their impending doom.

Rupert kept going on and on in a rather loud child's voice, "Mom, what if there was an earthquake right now and all of the stuff on those shelves started falling on us? What if hot lava came, would it come inside this store? Where would we go?"

As I pushed my bunker's worth of food down the aisles, I tried to distract him by bringing up dinosaurs, but that only led to their eventual destruction and brought him right back to the topic of impending doom.

I thought, "Okay, he wants to talk about a subject he finds fascinating. So what? I don't know these people. Let him talk. Let him ask questions." And then I hid behind the tower of canned soup on my cart, looking out from behind only long enough to make sure I was traveling in the right direction and no obstacles were in my path. Maybe nobody would see me. I would be the invisible cart driver. Next time, I will bring sunglasses and a wig.

▦　▦　▦

I have been told that it is important to use appropriate technical terms for personal body parts so that my children will not treat the subject as taboo or something to be ashamed of. Looking back a number of years, I tried this with my oldest son Stanley when he was only three. I soon learned, however, in one of the most embarrassing moments I can recall, that perhaps this wasn't such a good idea, because tact and discretion are not the better part of a young child's social skills. Young children often master certain social niceties such as being cute, but they don't often recognize that asking the waiter in technical terms about his private parts as he serves you your meal is not generally acceptable, even if you *are* only three years old. It will not only give parents a sudden case of the squirm-and-slide-under-the-table tremors, but it will cause the poor waiter to turn beet red and shift uncomfortably on his feet while he stutters something about refilling your glasses.

My next four children were taught the less proper terms once we got past arms, legs, fingers, and toes. I was willing to live with this temporary dumbing down on my conscience if it meant that we could spare just one waiter a little future embarrassment. For the longest time, Rupert thought he was blessed with two belly buttons. He asked me one day, "Mom, why do we have leaking parts of our bodies?"

He has it all figured out now.

⊞ ⊞ ⊞

That reminds me. One of the stories that I love comes from Corrie Ten Boom's book *The Hiding Place*. She talks about a time when she was 10 years old and she was riding the train with her father. She asked him about sex. Her normally responsive and instructive father didn't reply to her question, and she was a little put off by this. Then, on the way out of the train, her father asked her to grab his bag for him. She tried, but she couldn't lift it. He picked it up with what appeared to be ease. After they were off the train, he took her aside and said, "Corrie, there are some things that are too heavy for you to carry right now, but when you are older, you will be better able to bear the load." She realized he was talking about her question. He wasn't avoiding it. He wasn't intending on withholding that information forever, but he wanted her to understand that her little brain wasn't at a maturity level yet to handle all of the information she wanted. He also reassured her that when it was, he would be there with the necessary information.

Now I'm not saying that 10 is too young for any child to learn about the facts of life, but for some it may be. And some kids might be able to handle the technical terms of body parts at an early age without embarrassing unsuspecting strangers.

However, it is wise to remember that just because a child's brain is capable of *remembering* the information, it does not mean that child is capable of fully *understanding* the information or the responsibility that the information carries with it.

⊞ ⊞ ⊞

Rupert has at least some understanding of the burden of responsibility that can come when one knows something one is not supposed to know. At his Valentine's party in first grade, a little girl handed him an envelope that said, "From your secret admirer," and this was followed by her name.

As Rupert was relating this story to me, he said, "She didn't know what 'secret admirer' meant, so I just erased her name for her."

"Oh," I said, "Who was it?"

"I don't know," he answered. Yes, he's learning about being discreet with his relationships *and* his information.

⊞ ⊞ ⊞

I want to feed my children a healthy and well-balanced diet of information. I don't want to underestimate their ability to retain and use knowledge, but I want to carefully consider the information that they have access to at each stage of life, allowing them to carry more and more weight and responsibility of knowing things as they grow and mature.

Talking with our children is a terrific way to relay information and to make sure that it is understood properly. We are one of their best resources, and certainly as adults, we need the information they have to offer us as well. We want to know what they are thinking about, what is important to them, what worries them, and what is happening in their lives.

When our kids are younger, they often seem open with their feelings. Two-year-olds will let you know in no uncertain terms exactly how they feel. They will usually open up in the middle of an aisle of the grocery store and express their innermost thoughts at the top of their lungs. This is probably the pinnacle of communication in a child's life. After the temper tantrum stage, after they have learned to control their emotions a little more—or at least the expression of their emotions—and to delay gratification a bit more, they begin to realize that some of their thoughts can be kept to themselves. As they grow older, they reserve more and more of their thoughts and feelings, sharing them only with best friends or adults they trust. By the time they become teenagers, they may only express their feelings in unfathomable, explosive, and incomprehensible bursts of moodiness. Parents are left trying to decipher clues that would baffle even Sherlock Holmes.

But don't despair. I have discovered a way to get them to talk. I have come up with three techniques that I would like to share with you to help you get your teens to talk to you. Trust me, these work.

1. Buy yourself a really good book. Suspense works best, but anything you are intensely interested in will do. Let that book sit on your nightstand until a convenient opportunity arises and you have enough quiet time to get to it. (This should take at least a good week and a half.) Get comfortable, curl up on the couch or in bed, pick up the book and begin to read, and ta da! The moment you hit a particularly suspenseful section of the book, your teenager will magically appear, and words will spill out of his or her mouth for what seems like hours. This method is even more effective when you check your book out of the library rather than purchasing it—the urgency of the due date helps.

2. Teenagers are more prone to talk when several other people are talking at the same time. They are drawn into other people's conversations by some mystical and irresistible force called "competing for attention." For example, when the younger children come home from school and have a million things they want to say, the teenager in the group will suddenly find that his jaw has been

oiled and will spill out everything you ever wanted to know (which really isn't all that much, after all) about his life, and then will become irritated because you aren't listening. However, if you try to get him to talk to you about his day and there is no other competition around for background noise, he'll clam up in silence. The skill you must develop here is to be able to keep track of several different conversations at once, along with head-shaking skills and a vocabulary of noncommittal all-purpose words and phrases such as "Oh, really?" and "Huh!" while simultaneously making mental notes of the interesting tidbits you may want to follow up on later.

3. The third and last method is definitely the easiest, but painful. It is this. Get yourself exhausted. Wear yourself out. Don't sleep for three days. Teenagers have a way of sensing this in a parent, and it is their favorite time to open up and want to talk. For example, if you've only had three hours of sleep in the last four days and your alarm is set for 5:00 A.M., your teenager will wander in at about 2:30 A.M. and chat like there's no tomorrow. Believe me, I've been there. The hitch? Well, besides lack of coherent brain cells during waking hours, snoring can be a conversation stopper—though it doesn't always work. And sometimes, you can't remember everything that was said, especially those promises you might have made that you didn't mean to make and that you wouldn't have ever made if you had been in your right mind and fully cognitive.

I told you I've had to develop some creative coping strategies.

※ ※ ※

A steady supply of age-appropriate information is a must for the growing brain, and the brain growing at a high rate of speed is going to need more of it. But the information needs to go both ways. As parents, we want to supply *and* demand, or at least encourage. Just like our children, when we have the necessary information, we can make better decisions—whether it's about our children's educational needs, their emotional needs, or our relationships with them.

And just like our children, we also have to make sure that we are responsible and mature enough to handle the information we have been given. We don't want to share it with others or bring it up at the wrong times, like the time Stanley embarrassed the poor waiter. In fact, even though I share a lot of stories about my children and my siblings when I write, believe it or not, I'm holding some of the best stuff back. There are some stories I don't have permission to tell.

We have to sift through the information we have access to and decide which should be passed on and shared, which should be kept to ourselves, and which is harmful and best left alone. Faulty, inaccurate, or biased information may cause more harm than good.

When we have the proper information, we are better problem solvers. Maintaining an informed mind is a necessary coping skill. Pass it on.

4: They Are Way Ahead of Us

When my brother Myron and his wife were expecting their fourth child, the ever-mischievous Myron told his six-year-old son Harvey all sorts of things about what the new baby would be like. He said it would cry a lot and would have six toes.

Imagine Myron's surprise when little Bertie was born, and lo and behold, he did cry a lot—and amazingly enough, he *did* have six toes! Myron has learned not to make such predictions anymore. Little Bertie got the best of him. I have a feeling that he will grow up to be even more mischievous than his dad. Bertie will take his dad's gift and build upon it.

Kids are like that. It's kind of scary. You think, "Wow, kids these days are so smart!" And then those same kids grow up and have children and say to themselves, "Holy cow, kids these days are so smart!" I know this happens, because I remember. I remember being much smarter than my own parents. I think, however, that they may have caught up with me again. I know my teenagers think I'm not the brightest bulb of the bunch, and I'm beginning to think they're right. Having teenagers is one way to discover how little you know.

I also remember being smarter than my teachers. I used to get irritated to no end during those days when I sat at my desk and listened to my teacher read a story out loud to the class. For Pete's sake, she was pronouncing the names all wrong! This was particularly frustrating as I was too shy too correct her (which was probably for the best), and so I had to sit and suffer in silence. Now that I am an adult, I feel as though I have lost my edge. I am insecure about reading books aloud to my kids, because when I run into an unusual last name, I just know I'm going to pronounce it wrong and my kids will be correcting me in their heads.

I don't know if kids just *seem* to be smarter, if they *are* truly smarter, or if we as adults just let our brains wear down with use. (I think we must reach our mental peak at 18 and then begin the slow descent into mental a"dull"t-hood.) But I do know this: The kids are way ahead of us, and it's really annoying. They can out-argue us, out-reason us, outlast us. They ask questions we can't answer, and they can sometimes answer our questions for us. They remember every little thing—as long as that memory works to their advantage and doesn't have anything to do with chores or homework. They remember promises we don't remember making. They predict our behaviors and out-maneuver us. You know what? I think they read our minds. Yes. In fact, they may even be astute enough to practice mind control on us without our realizing what is happening. Kids are taking over the world. Buwahahahaha!

And when they are intellectually or creatively gifted, watch out. You don't have a chance. Just stand back and accept your fate.

⊞ ⊞ ⊞

For a long time, I drove the ugliest green minivan under the sun. Thanks to years of traveling up and down washboard roads, and more recently, being on the losing end of a deer who wandered out on the highway (more about the deer later), I was traveling in a squeaking, grunting vehicle with no rearview mirror, a missing taillight, a door that would hardly open, and dents all along one side. I was okay with it, because it was always easy to spot in a crowded parking lot, and I need all of the help I can get with those kinds of things. When we finally broke down (before our van did) and decided to buy a new minivan, my hubby and I took Pandora and Rupert with us to the car lot. Big mistake. Kids are more convincing than salesmen. When the salesman left my hubby and me alone to chat about the minivan we were considering, he probably knew the sale was his, because his two best weapons, Pandora and Rupert, were there to watch over and guide the outcome of the conversation. When my hubby expressed reservations over the price, Rupert said in a dramatic, low voice reminiscent of Obi Wan Kenobi, "Dad, it's your de-e-e-e-stiny!"

How could we turn down "the voice"?

The minivan was ours.

⊞   ⊞   ⊞

My mother Myrna is a diabetic with high blood pressure and a few other health issues. She is supposed to follow a fairly strict diet. If it were up to her, she would follow the diet maybe once a day for an hour or two. Fortunately, Myrna is not alone. She is almost never alone. Five-year-old Fritzie is her shadow and her dietician. Every time Myrna attempts to plop a tasty morsel of something or other in her mouth, Fritzie will shout out, "No, Grandma! That has fat in it!" Or sugar, or too much salt. Fritzie has most foods memorized. The only way Myrna can get away with anything is to hide in her room or lie about the foods that Fritzie is not yet familiar with. Fritzie has taken it upon herself to keep her grandma healthy, and she's going to keep her on the straight and narrow, by golly! Our kids have us in the palms of their hands. Oh sure, they let us think we're in control, that we have some ability to manage our families. They display the proper amount of dismay at a time-out or loss of privileges, but really, they've got us right where they want us.

The other day, she sat on my mom's lap as they both waited for a website that Fritzie enjoys to pop up on the screen. For some reason, it was taking an unusual amount of time to load.

My mom got bored, so she began to tickle Fritzie's sides while they waited.

Fritzie gave her a serious look. "Focus, Grandma. Focus."

🏵 🏵 🏵

Kids not only recognize their intuitive and cognitive superiority, they patronize us in their minds and sometimes make the mistake of expressing it. (Okay, maybe I'm being a little paranoid.) When my sister Edna dropped her daughter Wilhelmina off at first grade, she gave her a hug and a kiss and waved goodbye as her older daughter made her way to the school building. However, from the back seat, Fritzie, who was only three then, watched the scene unfold with her wise little three-year-old eyes. She giggled and said. "That's so *cute*. It's just like something on a TV show!"

Fritzie doesn't miss a thing. I was on a shopping trip with Edna and Darleen one day, and Darleen had the good fortune to sit in the back, next to Fritzie in her car seat. Darleen forgot that Fritzie was watching, and she did something that Edna wouldn't want Fritzie to do—she wrote a note on her hand. "Oops, sorry," Darleen said.

Fritzie leaned over and whispered, "It's okay. Just tell her it was an accident."

How old did I say she was? Three? She sounded like about 12 that time.

Yes, Fritzie has the big people in her world all figured out. She always has. When she was just a tiny baby, we all thought she looked so peaceful, just staring at us the way she did with hardly a peep out of her. Little did we know she was sizing us up and scoping out our weaknesses. When she was a toddler, like most other toddlers, she was into everything, but not in an impulsive way. No, it was clear she had a plan. She would distract whatever responsible adult happened to be around, probably known to her as "Obstacle A," and then proceed immediately to a chair that she had previously placed in front of the fish tank to grab a fish, or she'd go to someone's handbag to grab some gum. Her efficiency, speed, and frequent success suggested to us that she had preplanned her strategy, including her route. She not only had strategy, but she had perseverance. Even under the most watchful eye, she usually achieved her goal. If one distraction or route didn't work, she found another that would.

Now that she is five, Fritzie recognizes that some things are off limits, but she still remains keen and determined. She can outsmart any of us, and we all know it, which makes us extra vigilant. We always get the feeling that perhaps something is going on behind our backs (or even in front of our faces) to which we are completely oblivious. That sweet little sprite sitting on the couch may very well be distracting us with her innocent face while she is secretly operating a remote-controlled cookie grabber that she has designed for her cookie passion.

Okay, okay, I'm getting paranoid again, but I swear, when you see the gears turning in their little heads, it makes you wonder. Just when you think you're working with a typical five-year-old brain, the child in question will prove to you that you have no idea what a five-year-old brain is really capable of.

⊞　⊞　⊞

When Rupert was four or five and couldn't grasp the concept of "tomorrow," I wasn't particularly worried or surprised. I mean, I can understand struggling with a word that represents a time that is always on the horizon but never actually appears, even if the event that it is supposed to bring with it arrives anyway. Rupert is just a kid. He doesn't have all of the wisdom and experience necessary to grasp all of those complicated ideas. Right?

Right. Then how come he is still way ahead of me?

When he was four, Rupert memorized his favorite cousin Parker's phone number so he could call and invite himself over to play, or at least hint strongly, hoping for an invitation to Parker's house. I figured that since Rupert was capable of memorizing phone numbers, perhaps he ought to learn his own. However, he had no interest in doing so.

I said, "Rupert, you need to know your own phone number. What if something happened to you? What if you get lost and you need to tell someone so they can call us and tell us where you are?"

Rupert shrugged his shoulders. "If I get lost, I'll call Parker."

Okay. One point for Rupert. Zero for me. Even after five kids, I'm still at zero. The minute I think I've outplayed and outsmarted one of my children, I discover it is only a temporary illusion. I have yet to make the scoreboard.

In fact, when it comes to games, you know, like checkers or Clue or whatever, I'm a pretty competitive momma. Hubby likes to play to let the younger kids have a better chance, and he's even willing to throw the game if he thinks it's necessary, but when I play, it's no holds barred. I figure, hey, this is reality. When my children play against other kids, those kids aren't going to go easy on them, and my kids shouldn't expect to win every game they play. Besides, if their skills are going to improve, they need to be challenged.

That's what I tell myself, but the fact of the matter is if they really want a challenge, they should go find other kids to play with them, because they're not learning anything by beating me all the time.

⁂

I've heard of other parents who have mentally outmaneuvered their children on occasion, and I take comfort in knowing that it's possible. So far, I haven't had much luck. My sister does better with it.

One Christmas, Darleen told her two oldest children, Calvin and Luella, that the presents for their cousins were being stored at her house and that she had agreed to make sure they were wrapped and ready for Christmas Eve. She then asked Calvin to wrap the boys' presents and Luella to wrap the girls' presents, which in reality were their own presents. So Calvin and Luella both fumed about how lucky their cousins were to get every-thing that they themselves had wanted. They wrapped and packed the presents away in their mom's closet and then spent the next few weeks searching everywhere else in the entire house and turning it inside out looking for their own presents. Darleen didn't have a lot of storage space; she needed to get cre-ative about keeping the surprise alive for Christmas. Imagine the surprise on her children's faces when they saw the presents they had wrapped under the tree on Christmas morning!

I am sitting here now lost in admiration for Darleen's simple genius. Some people would think it a mean trick, but after years of Calvin and Luella outsmarting her at every turn and discov-ering their gifts ahead of the big day, it was time to turn the tables. Still, it's the kind of thing you can do only once.

⌗ ⌗ ⌗

Christmas is one of the toughest times of the year to get away with secrets. Pandora and Magnolia both had the mythi-cal holiday characters figured out by the time they were four. Also the fairy that pays for teeth. I can't pull the wool over their eyes. Rupert is still a believer, though this last year, he had his questions. One night he insisted on knowing the truth, but when he could see that I was hesitant to tell him, he said, "Never mind, Mom, we can talk about it on Christmas morning." I was grateful that he was willing to give me one more year. I think he was testing things out, however, because he refused to tell anyone else but Santa what he wanted for Christmas. I kept asking him, since I didn't want a disappointed little boy on the morning of one of my favorite holidays. Finally he sighed and said, "Okay, I want Pokemon stuff and technology stuff."

Great. I could do that. No problem. However, when we went to the community Christmas event and Rupert sat on the Big Guy's lap, a friend overheard him whisper that what he really wanted was an X-Box.

Well, that was that. I was going to have a disappointed little boy on Christmas morning after all. So sad. Some things have to be learned the hard way.

Rupert is quick to question the adult world when he gets his suspicions. When he was in kindergarten, he tried out for a part in the *Snow White* production that the Children's Theater was presenting at our elementary school. He was given the part of a bat. The next day, he plopped a Little Golden Book of Disney's *Snow White* on my lap and said, "There are no bats in here." His eyes said, "Either they've given me a really lame part or someone is very confused. Maybe they've got their stories mixed up. Should we tell them?" He'd done his research. He wasn't simply going to take somebody else's word for something just because they were older and taller and had bat costumes.

☷ ☷ ☷

Anyway, while Rupert may not easily grasp some abstract ideas, there are other complicated ideas that he does pick up on. One day he was asking me about different countries and what makes them different besides their geography. Why are we divided into clusters of land space? He wanted to know. So I explained to him about different types of governments and the concept of freedom, because obviously he's never been exposed to anything else other than the sheltered life of a young kid. To him, freedom means that he doesn't have to clean his room that day and he can have all of the cookies and ice cream he wants.

A few days later, he and his older brother Stanley were arguing about the technical status of their friendship. Stanley claimed that they were best friends, while Rupert insisted that they were only good friends. Finally, after going back and forth about it for 15 minutes, Rupert became frustrated and decided to end it once and for all. He raised his voice and said, "Listen, Stanley, I'm the gov-er-ment!"

I believe he meant an authoritarian dictatorship with little or no ability to enforce its dictates. However, Stanley was satisfied. The issue was settled. And I was left with the impression that Rupert understood more about the government than I expected his young and inexperienced brain to grasp.

▦ ▦ ▦

We should not set unrealistic expectations on our children's abilities; neither should we set limits on the potential of those abilities. They're going to surprise you every time—and not just in our own families.

Six-year-old Imogene was in the middle of a conversation with an adult when the adult remarked, "My, you sure are articulate."

Imogene asked, "What does 'articulate' mean?"

"It means to understand words and know how to use them."

"Well," little Imogene said, "if I were really articulate, don't you think I would know what that word meant?"

Another time, Imogene was riding in the backseat as her mother drove past a Ronald McDonald house when she asked, "Mom, what is that house?"

Her mom answered, "Oh, that's a Ronald McDonald house. They provide a place to stay for families when their children are in the hospital."

"Oh." A few seconds later, Imogene piped up again, "Hey, wait a minute! Aren't those the people who keep feeding us the bad hydrogenated oils?"

Nobody is going to get past Imogene. Her six-year-old brain is operating at the speed of light. All the rest of us can do is watch her whiz by and wonder what just happened. She is the blur, the almost invisible burst of wind that whips by and leaves us reeling as we try to collect our thoughts and put the pieces back together again.

Then there's Javier. When little Javier was asked to bring one hundred of anything to first grade to help celebrate the one hundredth day of school, he showed up seemingly empty-handed. His teacher said, "Javier, how come you didn't bring in your assignment? Did you forget?"

"On no, Mrs. Gallawagger. They're all right here."

"Where? What are they?"

"Standing right here next to me. I brought one hundred invisible friends."

And sure enough, his one hundred invisible friends followed him around all day. I have a feeling the hallways were a little more crowded than usual.

🀫 🀫 🀫

I have to admit that even though it's intimidating to realize that I am in a constant state of being outsmarted by the young and supposedly innocent, I find it exciting, thrilling even, to watch their brains grasp ideas. I am amazed at the information they are able to retain and to process. Rupert is like a bubbling geyser, spewing out a constant stream of facts that he has memorized. "Hey, Mom, I'll bet that horse over there is a stallion."

"Why do you think that, Rupert?"

Because it's bigger than any horse I've ever seen, and stallions are big horses. Did you know a kid could go under a stallion without crawling?"

"Nope. I didn't know that. Where did you learn that?"

"My teacher told me."

He remembers *everything* his teacher tells him (with the exception of the instructions for his schoolwork). He seems to remember everything *anybody* tells him, plus incidental things he hears just out in the world, not necessarily from anyone talking to him. His sweet little nearly-toothless grin belies the amazing high-powered computer that hides underneath a shock of dirty blonde hair that is badly in need of a trim. That computer never shuts down—not even at night, when dreams take him on adventures to explore a world that is inaccessible to him in the daytime. I am in awe.

And other times I am in fear. The kids are way ahead of us, and sometimes they take advantage of this fact. And sometimes, they have a little fun with it—a little too much fun.

⊞ ⊞ ⊞

Darleen's son Calvin is at least as mischievous as his uncle Myron. When he was in sixth grade, he knew that his parents had invited the rest of the family over for a picnic. He's a pretty helpful kid, and so he was glad to help get the backyard ready for company. The table was set up under a tree, and chairs were placed around. Everyone arrived and seemed to be enjoying themselves until… until…his aunt looked up from the serving table and screamed. Calvin had loaded the undersides of the branches with dangling rubber snakes from his toy snake collection.

Who can let April Fool's Day pass by uncelebrated? Not Calvin. While his parents were still asleep, he crept into their bathroom and loaded his mom's toothbrush with adult Orajel. When she brushed her teeth the next morning, her mouth went so numb that she could hardly speak!

This is sometimes how life is when you live with a little person with an overactive brain. Kids take their imaginations and combine them with a little ingenuity and creativity to liven up their own lives and the lives of those lucky ones who live with them. As long as they don't overstep the bounds and leap into cruelty, destruction, or danger, this isn't such a bad thing. After all, they may grow up some day to have a bright future in the sitcom business. And at least life in a home with one of these individuals is never boring.

If you're the parent, the kids need to know that you can roll with the punches now and then. Sometimes, they'll even let you in on the fun. Join them. (Especially since you know you really can't beat them.)

⊞ ⊞ ⊞

My daughter isn't shy about recruiting help when necessary. Pandora is always looking for ways to "get" us. She is also one of those busy-brained kids who can't shut their minds down at night when it's time to go to sleep. I am forever telling her to put her book away (the book she is reading in the dark) and get some sleep—especially on school nights. I can pretty much count on at least one book every night. In fact, she often has several books hiding under her pillow or quilt. When she makes her bed, there are always a few square-shaped lumps under the covers.

One evening, after I had gotten after her two or three times already and removed at least one book, my husband came into our bedroom and said, "Pandora's at it again. She's reading past her lights-out time. What do you think we should do?"

"I have had it!" I gave a small growl, jumped up from my own comfy bed, and stomped into her room, Hubby following closely behind. My daughter lay there very still under her covers, but she couldn't fool me. (Well, okay, she had previously done so on many occasions, but I was temporarily out of my mind and suffering under the delusion that she couldn't fool me.) Pandora often pretended to be asleep, and I wasn't about to fall for it this time.

"Pandora?"

Oh, there it was—I saw her head flinch a little. Boy, was I on to her!

"Pandora, knock it off. I know you're not sleeping!"

Her head moved a bit again under the covers.

"That's enough, Pandora. Are you reading another book?"

She moved her head again. I figured she was trying to bury her face in her pillow so she could stifle her giggles. "Okay, that's enough, Pandora!" and I pulled the covers back to expose her wicked book-reading-in-the-middle-of-the-night-on-a-school-night.

There was no book! There was no Pandora either! There was, however, a balloon where her head should have been. A muffled laugh came out from under the bed. Even worse, there was a not-so-muffled laugh coming from my husband, who had been in on the joke from the beginning.

I stood there for a moment, dumbfounded, until Pandora's real head appeared from under the bed. She had been under there operating her balloon puppet head by pulling on its string to make it move.

I tried to save face as my anger deflated and a slight case of embarrassment took over. Then I felt a case of the giggles myself rising up from my stomach and trying to escape out of my mouth. I held them down for as long as I could, but within 15 seconds, they cut loose, out of my control. We all had a good infectious laugh—the kind where you can't stop laughing for a while.

Yes, she was way ahead of me. And you know what? I have to admit it was kind of fun. It was a good memory that we share between the three of us. It's okay to not always be the one who's right, the one who's ahead of the game, because there is joy in watching someone else, even when that someone else is younger and has no right to be smarter, exceed the mental expectations that have been set for them.

My husband and I both struggle to keep up with our children. He has suggested to me that we give them what he calls "pre-emptive time-outs," because we know they are always up to something, and we have no other way to head them off at the pass.

In reality, I think all we can do is set a foundation of rules to live by and then pull in the reins on occasion when those rules are being tossed aside. Other than that, we're going to just sit back and enjoy watching them run.

5: Getting It All Under Control

When my nephew Calvin was about eight years old, most of the family's socks went missing. Disappeared. They weren't in the drawers, and they weren't in the laundry. Just when Darleen was about ready to call in Encyclopedia Brown, she discovered the missing footwear in Calvin's room.

All of the sock hogging had nothing to do with warming his cold feet; it had to do with an empty wallet—Calvin needed a little extra cash. He had taken the socks and turned them all into sock puppets to sell door-to-door in the neighborhood. Darleen had a little chat with Calvin about using things that didn't belong to him, and no, that didn't mean he could turn all of his own socks into sock puppets, either. Together they disassembled the puppets, pulling off eyeballs and pompom noses, and put the socks back in the drawers where they belonged.

Calvin's dad wasn't especially thrilled about wearing black socks with stiff, fuzzy, pink spots on the toes to work, but at least he had a good story to tell. In our family, we thrive on good stories. It's another one of our survival techniques.

Calvin's creativity and resourcefulness was really a good thing, but he didn't consider the consequences. His goal was to earn money. He wasn't thinking about causing a fuzzy footwear shortage. He had a goal, and that was all he could see.

🆙 🆙 🆙

There are times when it is easy for me to believe that some of my children have no goals. Stanley scored exceptionally high on every test he ever took that measured his intelligence or his abilities, and yet none of this showed up in his school career. He decided to give college a try, which lasted exactly one semester, because it felt too much like school. Now, almost two years later, he has changed his tune. He *wants* to go to school. He can't wait to get back, and he's saving his paychecks to fund his own education.

Magnolia brings home report cards that I'd like to slip under a couch cushion and forget about. She passed English this year only because her teacher was kind enough to give her a second chance to turn in her missing assignments at the last minute and allow her to retake a test or two. Yet out of all of the freshmen in her high school class, Magnolia has the second highest reading score on the state achievement test. She's capable, but she chooses not to live up to her capabilities. It is a choice. School, for one reason or another, just isn't important to her. I might worry about her work ethic, but then she got a job at a restaurant and was named Employee of the Month after her first month there. She takes her job seriously and has no patience for those who slack off and get paid "to just stand around" or who pretend to look busy. She has goals. Getting good grades is not one of them. She wants to decide for herself what is important.

Sometimes, especially with gifted people, the intensity of their characteristics determines their goals, and they miss the rest of the picture. These wonderful characteristics—like curiosity, creativity, and focus—are good things, exciting things, but they still require a little self-discipline, as well as an ability to see the bigger picture. You can't play a musical instrument well without some practice, yet if you spend too many hours practicing, you might neglect other things that are important. You can't be an electrician without getting certification, no matter how smart you are or how interested you are in pursuing that career. Not every player who dreams of it will make the NBA. Kids don't often have the bigger picture; adults have to gently help.

⊞　⊞　⊞

My sister Hortense is a stubborn…no, let's call her a *persistent* person. She sees what she wants, and she won't let go of it. This is a good thing. She knows what she wants. She achieves that goal. If only all of us could be so efficient! As an adult, Hortense has learned how to harness her determination and make it work for her. However, as a 17-year-old, she was right there in the car with my parents when they went out to celebrate their anniversary—and she chose the restaurant for them. Hey, she was hungry, and she knew what she wanted. She saw her goal. She didn't necessarily see my parents' goal—which was a nice romantic evening *alone*.

Now my parents may seem like pushovers for letting her go along, and even more for letting her call the shots, but things aren't always what they seem. Hortense was *determined*. She could have found her way through a maze blindfolded and with both hands tied behind her back if she knew her goal was at the other end. Two parents who wanted to be alone was only a minor obstacle for her. Pshaw! Child's play.

Magnolia is equally as determined. My husband says that one of his best defense methods to save himself from Magnolia's "convincing sessions" is to pretend that he's asleep. And if he needs to go to the grocery store, I try to distract her while he sneaks out. Otherwise she'll give him a list of the groceries that she thinks we really *need*. I look at her and ask myself how I can help her to channel her energy into achieving positive goals without taking off the edge, and therefore the strength, of her determination. I want her to reach adulthood with all of her precious persistence intact, but I still have to help her learn how to harness her energy.

⊞　⊞　⊞

The intensity that giftedness brings with it is only a gift if a person can get it under control and use it wisely. This is no simple feat. Intensity in its natural state isn't a tame animal. And we don't really want to tame it anyway; we just want to channel it and guide it.

When I say "we," I mean the adults responsible for young, rapid traveling brains, but mostly "we" means parents and teachers. We need to learn to control and guide our intensities ourselves. Our children will learn from our modeling to do the same thing.

My parents, and really, probably mostly Myrna, needed to learn to control their intense curiosity at Christmastime, because every Christmas morning, we children woke up to used toys. You see, my parents couldn't resist testing things out and putting them together and seeing how they worked. When I opened up a new set of Legos, there was a half-constructed house in the box. None of our toys were shrink-wrapped by the time we got to them. Apparently, Santa and his elves didn't believe in that kind of thing. I have visions in my head, not of dancing sugarplums, but of two grown adults sitting under the tree playing Rock 'Em, Sock 'Em Robots. I guess they couldn't help themselves.

🔳 🔳 🔳

Intensity can flare up in a variety of ways. Any fast brain or talent area can be taken to an extreme. My daughter Pandora needs to get her intense desires for perfectionism, coupled with her intense imagination, under control. For a while, when she would go to bed at night, she couldn't breathe well, and she would panic. Asthma runs in the family, so I treated her accordingly. However, after talking to someone else who had a child with similar symptoms, I realized that she could be reacting to her fears of failing and the horrors of falling short as they played out in her imagination. As her thoughts ran out of control, which was mostly at night when she couldn't sleep and her brain had lots of free time to explore all of the possibilities in her life, her throat tightened up, and this scared her even more, so the situation only got worse.

I discussed my theory with her, and she agreed that it was probably what was happening. We decided that the best thing to do was to take her mind off her troubles before she went to bed. She needed a distraction, so I gave up the no-books-in-the-middle-of-the-night rule for a while and let her read until she was sleepy enough to pass out. (Yes, she won. She got to read in bed at night. I'm telling you, I can't keep up with them! But it helped another problem, and that was important.) She didn't necessarily learn how to banish her intense worries, but she learned how to manage them. She learned to set them aside or put them to sleep so she could get some sleep herself.

After a while, Pandora was able to go to sleep without her books. She has quelled, at least temporarily, those worries and learned how to relax her breathing, as well as her brain. She knows how to handle the situation on her own. She understands what is happening. She has exercised some control over the situation.

Ultimately, that's the goal for all of us—to learn how to manage our passions and our weaknesses and channel them in a beneficial direction. Pandora is one step closer to doing so. But first, she had to gain an understanding of the problem before she could take steps to resolve it.

❇   ❇   ❇

Gifted imaginations and extreme sensitivities can often blow reality out of proportion and send it flying into the dark recesses of space.

I myself have an incredible ability to imagine the worst-case scenario in any given situation. This is not a pleasant gift to have. I have to rein it in and control it, or I could end up like Howard Hughes, believing that the world is full of frightening things and living like a hermit to avoid those frightening things. When I find myself thinking about what *could* have happened in any given situation, I have to stop my brain in its tracks and focus on something else to get those frightful images off the stage of my mind. When I think about what *can* happen, I have to take a deep breath and just trust that the end of the world isn't going to happen right this moment, and then I cross my fingers for good measure. When my children are climbing trees or driving on their own for the first time, I have to find a distraction. That is usually the answer I give to my children when they are afraid or in pain: "Think about something else."

I am a notorious chicken. You can guess most of my fears. Sharks. Heights. Spiders. Mountain lions. I used to be afraid to take a shower after Jaws came out, because water of any kind, even the sprinkling-over-my-head kind, was enough to trigger grisly sea life episodes in my imagination. I hate watching scary movies—even the most ridiculously unbelievable ones—because even though I can walk away from the movie in a perfectly sane state of mind, mocking the creator of such ridiculous nonsense, later that evening I'll begin to see imaginary things out of the corner of my eye. I've heard that Stephen King is a master of scary plots. I wouldn't know. I can't even bring myself to open one of his books. His name alone is enough to conjure up images of potentially frightening scenarios.

When I was a kid, we had this amazing set of animal encyclopedias. I loved them—they were so full of information and pictures! But I had to turn the pages with my fingernails, because I couldn't bear the thought of my skin accidentally touching the picture of a tarantula or a snake. I have since outgrown this particular fear, but my imagination is still alive and well, and when it finds other minds with similar imaginations? Well, let's just say we're all in trouble.

One night, I was sitting out on our front deck with my sister Gertrude and her husband Ignatius watching a meteor shower. We'd been there for a while, and our necks were developing some serious cricks.

I said, "You know what? If we go out to the backyard, we can all sit in the cushioned swing and recline so that we can stare up at the sky without straining our necks."

They agreed that it was a fine idea, so we did just that. The swing was much more comfortable, and we sat there for about five minutes when an ugly thought crept into my mind. You need to know here that we live in the foothills of some mountains in Montana.

"Uh, guys? I just realized that we have our backs to the hillside and the trees, and it's pitch black, and mountain lions like to hunt at night, and they attack from behind."

Ignatius responded, "Huh."

We sat there in silence for about 30 more seconds. Then, without anyone saying another word, we all jumped up at the same time and ran back into the house.

I'm proud to say I was the first one to reach the patio door. Unfortunately, Gertrude and Ignatius were right behind me, and I had been running so fast that I didn't pause to note that the screen door was shut. I ran smack into it and then was mashed into it twice more as my two relatives smacked into me. I had a lovely imprint of the screen door on the tip of my nose, but fortunately, no one was seriously hurt, and we foiled the plans of any potentially hungry mountain lions.

I used to live in fear of mountain lions and grizzly bears even during the day, but then I began a pathetic and amateurish, though highly satisfying, attempt at gardening. It was difficult at first, to step outside all alone and turn my back to the trees while I popped carrot seeds into the soil, but gradually, as I realized that nothing terrible had happened thus far, I began to get over it. I worked my way through it, sort of. I still turn my head every time I hear the snap, crackle, and drop of a pine cone fluttering down through the branches and landing on the ground behind me. And I must confess that every once in a while, I look up and gaze at the seven-foot wire grid fence that my husband put up to keep the deer out, and I ask myself, "Could a mountain lion jump that? Could a grizzly bear push it over? What's my best escape route? Is there anything I can throw?"

Okay, Karen. Think of something else. Get it under control. Don't let your imagination run away with your sanity.

And the truth is, of course, that most of the time, I am grateful for my imagination. It takes me to a lot of really cool places. I have dreams, and sometimes, when I imagine them in great detail, it's enough to get me through, even when those dreams don't immediately come true.

⊞ ⊞ ⊞

Speaking of dreams, a few years ago, we had plans to sell our home and build my dream house—a small Victorian mansion. Okay, well, not really a mansion, but Victorian anyway. I spent hours lying in bed when I should have been sleeping, visualizing the wallpaper and the windows and the arched doorway, and plotting how I would arrange for some stained glass in the windows. In meetings, when I should have been listening, I imagined the wood flooring and the window treatments and the way my office would be set up. I knew which dishes went in which cupboards. I had every detail figured out. Heck, I practically lived there.

The house never came to pass—not in the world of reality, at least not yet. A business venture changed our plans. But guess what—I was okay with that, because I'd already lived in that house anyway. I had mentally designed it and spent many a day there. I'd experienced Christmas mornings, Halloween trick-or-treaters, and Thanksgiving dinners with family in that house. I was satisfied.

I'd still love to have that house, should the opportunity arise, but it isn't as urgent now as it was. My imagination has satisfied that yearning in me.

My imagination fuels my creativity, which is the thing that keeps me breathing with excitement every day—whether I'm sitting at my computer concocting a story for a novel, or sitting in my project room attempting another painting. Imagination helps my garden grow, at least in my head, and maintains my enthusiasm for it, because I can still visualize good things—like plants that survive and even thrive.

My imagination shows me what is possible, for good or for ill, and all I need to do is learn to manage it. No small feat, but doable. I'd rather keep it and accept the pain than lose it and lose the wonder and creativity.

🔡 🔡 🔡

Imagination and creativity may require a little corralling at times. When my mother and her friend decided to make potato candy (this was during my mom's worst let's-get-creative-with-food phase, as demonstrated with her pea bread), they didn't just make one batch. Nope. My mom figured that since she was going to have to boil potatoes for this concoction, she might as well boil a whole pot full. They used every last potato, and they made every flavor and every color of potato candy known to man—and even some that weren't.

This is when they ran into a problem. Potato candy, at least the stuff they made, turned out to have a disgusting taste. Now they had a new problem. How do you get rid of several pounds of potato candy? You can't just throw it away, not when there are people who are starving. So after trying to convince us kids to eat up, to no avail, my mom packaged it and insisted that we deliver it to the neighbors and take it to school to share with our friends, which was a perfectly good plan to make sure we didn't have any—friends, that is. I suppose her conscience would rest easier if someone else threw it away and she didn't have to know about it. So somewhere in North Idaho, someone someday will find an old landfill full of toxic waste—fermented potato candy in every flavor and every color known to man.

🔡 🔡 🔡

Sometimes, even when imagination or creativity is running along healthy lines, it can be a distraction that keeps the creator from other important tasks.

Rupert's creative juices have been focused in a robot phase for as long as he's known that such amazing things as robots existed. When I walk into his room at night, he is likely to be there, staring at the ceiling in the dark. He'll chirp up, "Mom, I'm going to build an Easter-egg-coloring robot. You'll be able to put the egg in over here, and then, brrrrrp, it'll come out whatever color you want it over here. And it will…."

There was a time when his whole life was robots. That was the only place his brain would take him. When he began kindergarten, he knew he had friends, but he couldn't remember what their names were. I told him to find out. But every day when he came home, he would say something like, "I tried to find out today and pay attention, but I was accidentally thinking about robots again and I forgot." His imagination is as active as my own—in fact, probably more so.

I can relate to his preoccupation with things that aren't real yet. Does he need to train his brain to set those things aside every once in a while and pay attention to his reading assignment? Well, yes. That would be a good plan. It'll probably take some time, though. I have yet to master it myself. And, if he's like me, Rupert will also need to learn to manage the imaginative fears he experiences. Now that he's seven, he still won't go into the basement by himself, even though it's a nice, bright, daylight sort of basement where we all spend a lot of our time. He doesn't like being alone, period. His imagination takes over and runs away with his courage.

There are many other examples of quick-brain characteristics that become strengths run amok. I'm sure you can think of a few yourself. The world is full of examples.

☷ ☷ ☷

My niece Gabby is an artist. When she was five, her mom would set paper plates on the table for dinner, turn her back to stir the stroganoff, and then turn back around to find that Gabby had already drawn on every single plate on the table. To young and passionate artists, every surface represents a new possibility. The living room wall is merely a canvas waiting for crayons. The trick is to teach these artists how to control their artistic impulses without tamping them down into the ground. They need opportunity and guidance, and hey, paper plates seem like a perfectly good opportunity.

⊞　⊞　⊞

Pandora loves to read, and she loves to accomplish things. These are both good skills to have. However, when she asks me to bring her to school early so she can take 10 Accelerated Reader tests in one morning, I start to wonder. Is her intense desire to succeed creeping beyond manageable boundaries? Is it going to interfere with her sleep again?

Giftedness is like that. Each characteristic (intensity, passion, curiosity, idealism, etc.) has a dark side, but it also has the capacity to bring incredible joy into one's life. The sensitive mind may be subject to depression on dark, cloudy days, but it can also revel in a sunset and find overwhelming happiness in something as simple as frothy hot cocoa in a styrofoam cup. An unusually alert and aware mind can be weighed down by the nightly news, but it can also savor every detail of a well-constructed poem or view the rules of physics as a thing of beauty. Passion may tempt one to neglect the usual and necessary routines of daily life, but it may also drive one to astounding discoveries.

These gifts are like a hammer—you can pound in a nail with it and build a house, or you can use it to smash in a window. Like any tool, it has potential for good or ill, depending on how it's used. It's all about understanding how to use it effectively and getting it under control.

⊞　⊞　⊞

Rupert is an intense little person who wears his heart on his sleeve. He needs a constant display of love, and he is conscientious about giving that love back. He can't stand anyone laughing at him—it hurts him deeply. When he is happy, he is really happy, but when he is miserable, watch out!

We discovered this past year that a full day of school is enough to exhaust Rupert. He comes home every day worn out, grumpy, whiny, and complaining. The minute he gets a chance to sit still, he starts snoring. Originally, his bedtime was 8:00 P.M., so I moved it up an hour to 7 P.M. Even though he hated going to bed early, it seemed to work well, because the moment he hit the pillow, he was out like a light.

A couple of weeks ago, he came home from school in great spirits. I asked him to clean his room, which normally brings a reaction of shock and dismay, even though this is a daily request and by now he should be expecting it. I usually get a whine and a complaint, but on this day, I got a "Yes, Mother!" I thought, "Hmmm. That's nice for a change."

When he and Pandora got into a tussle, I said, "Rupert, please get away from Pandora's room."

Instead of saying, "But I didn't do anything!" he said, "Okay, Mom."

Was this a new Rupert? I wondered what was going on.

Later that evening, when I asked him to sweep the hallway entrance, he said, "I'd be delighted to, Mother!" and he immediately went to work.

Just a sec, let me replay those words for my own benefit... "immediately went to work." Oh, that feels good. The typical response when I ask my children to do something is, "Okay, in a minute." This is their way of stalling until I forget that I have asked them.

Okay, back to Rupert. I wasn't sure what had gotten into him, so I asked, "What's gotten into you?"

"I'm trying to earn my old bedtime back."

"Oh, I see. I like that idea."

"Hey, Mom, how about this—how about if I don't earn my bedtime back for good, but I only earn it back on the days I'm not grumpy?"

"I like that idea even better."

Rupert has been holding himself together for several days now. He checks the whining and the complaining as soon as he catches it coming out of his mouth. Early stages of self-discipline seem to be settling in.

I think Rupert is way ahead of me on this one, too!

6: Living in the Real World

One day last summer, Otto, Magnolia, Pandora, Rupert, and I were gathered in the kitchen for lunch when Otto called our attention to a scene of drama and suspense—and it was playing out right above our heads in the skylight. A spider had planted itself in the corner of the skylight while a daredevil of a fly repeatedly zipped down at it and back up again as though it were taunting the earthbound arachnid. We forgot our peanut butter and jelly for the moment and craned our necks back to enjoy the show. The fly repeatedly dove at the spider, flirting with death. Whether it was a matter of clueless insect stupidity or an act of heroic buggy daredevil narcissism, we didn't know. As my kids watched, full of morbid curiosity, I watched them. They reminded me of the ancient Romans rooting for a man taking on a lion in our skylight coliseum.

Six-year-old Rupert began chanting, "Fight…Fight…Fight…."

And I thought, "This is what qualifies as entertainment at our house. This is what happens because we don't have satellite TV."

❁   ❁   ❁

Sometimes I look at my family, both my immediate family and my extended family, and wonder, "Do other people live like this? Or is it just us?"

It can't be just us, I think, because I've heard other stories a lot like ours. What about the woman whose father wore a clown costume for her wedding photos? I *know* we're not totally alone!

But sometimes it doesn't seem as if we're living in the real world with the rest of the seemingly normal and sensible people, either. I suppose it's our own fault, all of us oddities. I mean, we try to blend in and at least look normal. We wear somewhat normal clothing, at least most of the time. Our peculiarities leak out every now and then, but the public is usually (with the exception of certain cases like the clown apparel in the wedding photos) unaware of the full extent of our quirks and eccentricities. My book *Raisin' Brains* was my "coming out" with my family's weirdness, revealing our full identity while hoping that "the nice young men in the clean white coats" didn't come to take us away.

It seems we do things differently—at least some of the time. Oh sure, we still wear socks (though there's no guarantee that they always match), and we drive cars (I use the term "drive" here loosely), and we eat with spoons, forks, and knives (or utensils of our own invention) just like everyone else. But there is definitely something different happening in our house.

Or maybe not. Maybe a lot of other people are weird like us and just afraid to admit it. It is certainly possible that we're all suffering from the delusion that everyone else's family is "normal." Everyone has something to hide, I guess. Well, in our family, the skeleton in the closet is made up of funny bones and ticklish ribs and is wearing a fish tie and homemade underwear, and his bones have been reorganized to replace the missing pieces that have been pilfered for science experiences or unusual inventions.

Half of the time, we don't cook normal food, because our brains want to experiment. We don't even necessarily wake up the same way other people do. Rupert recently asked his dad to wake him up using a special contraption that he built for that purpose. His dad was supposed to place a marble in one end of the contraption, and it would eventually work its way through a Rube Goldberg maze type of thing, fall out, and land on Rupert's forehead. Fortunately, Rupert gave up on this idea before the thing was finished, or he might have ended up with a large permanent lump in the middle of his forehead and a bed full of marbles. By the way, in our house, making your bed means pulling the blanket and sheet over the top of whatever objects happen to be there, smoothing it out the best you can, and resting the pillow over the lumpiest parts. Make it work.

⊞   ⊞   ⊞

Rupert, maybe because he's the youngest, is a little peculiar. He fits right in with the rest of us, but he doesn't really live in the real world much. It's his imagination. He extends his world beyond the realm of normalcy and our quirky family and boldly goes where no brain has gone before. Just like with his robots, he spends most of his time in a galaxy far, far away. He came to me about a year ago with the statement, "Mom, I think I'm going to live on Mars, but first I have to plant some flowers there so I can breathe some good air."

A day or two later, he approached me with a handful of clothes hangers. "Do you know what these hangers are for, Mom? They're for my spaceship, because we're going to need hangers in space."

"That's nice, dear, but let's use them with your shirts in the bedroom closet for now."

Rupert is always planning, planning, planning for his next adventure, and I live in both fear and wonderment. He asked me in all seriousness the other day, "Mom, is it okay if Pandora and I start taking this house apart so we can build a time-travel ship?" And then he assured me, "Don't worry, because we're going to travel back to your childhood, so you'll still have a house. You can use your old one."

Then he asked if I had any "metal-melting tools to build a tank for the rockets," and, oh yeah, by the way, did I have any oil he could use?

You'll be reading about us in the news any day. Our house will either explode or it will disappear—one two-by-four at a time.

I didn't want to quash his dreams, but I'd sort of like to keep the house I have, so I mentioned that time-traveling spaceships made out of wood probably wouldn't survive the heat of re-entering the atmosphere. He would need lots of metal. I felt safe in saying this, because we don't have a lot of unused metal lying around. But then I realized that some morning I might wake up only to find that my stove has disappeared overnight.

I'm glad I didn't mention that the metal would need to be insulated, or I could wake up some morning to a very cold house with little telltale pieces of yellow fiberglass leading a trail to Rupert and Pandora's secret hide-out.

⊞ ⊞ ⊞

You know what a kid like Rupert wants for Christmas? An X-Box is nothing. The year before that, he asked for a rocket engine. He was as likely to get that as his cousin Fritzie was to get that dead elephant she asked for. Yes, she wanted a real one, though I have no idea why. Forget ponies and baby brothers. Try coming up with a dead elephant or a rocket engine. NASA doesn't have a discount outlet up in our neck of the woods, and we are also experiencing a dearth of dead elephants here in Montana.

⊞ ⊞ ⊞

When I was working on a sewing project and unraveling a bunch of gray threads, Rupert gathered them up and announced that he was saving them for his time-travel project. He said my husband would need them, because he, Rupert, would be traveling to the future, where his dad would have gray hair and look like the "Bush"—as in President Bush.

Rupert and Pandora have the time-travel thing all figured out. If you go back in time to a place where you already exist, then the future "you" is invisible. Rupert would like to visit himself as a baby in the hospital. He also wants to live in China "once that bird flu thing goes away." And if hot lava ever comes our way, Rupert has already declared that the first thing we need to save is the wires from our house. You can tell where his priorities are. Once, when he was sick with the flu, I sat up for most of the night with him to be sure his temperature stayed down. He kept me entertained with his sleepy conversation. Apparently, he also has plans to drain the water out of the Pacific Ocean by drilling a hole in the ocean floor near Hawaii. That's my boy—always the practical one.

⊞ ⊞ ⊞

Rupert may spend most of his time living in another reality, but the good news is that he plans on saving the "reald" (world) some day, so you can all breathe a huge sigh of relief now. Everything is going to be okay. Rupert's got it all under control.

One night, as he was staring out the window at the night sky, I asked him what was on his mind.

"Oh, I was just wishing on a star that the people in Zelda (a Nintendo game) were real so we could save the reald."

I overheard him talking to one of his friends on the phone the other day. "Do you want to be a ninja? Because I'm training ninja fighters, and it isn't just a game. It's for real."

He tells me that he's only training kids that he knows well. Perhaps that's a good idea. We can't take any chances that any of his well-trained ninjas will turn to the dark side. So far, he's recruited two friends, who, I'm sure, believe in the cause as much as he does. He's making a roster right now with a red magic marker on a yellow pad of lined paper. Everyone knows that rosters should look fancy and include thick red lines to separate the information, yes? Apparently that's a requirement.

Rupert is always starting clubs and recruiting other kids. He carries a notebook with him sometimes, and it contains all his "pryvit" plans. He took his journal to school and gathered his closest friends around him. Together, they mapped out their top secret Pokemon plans, starting with a village that they are going to build inside a mountain. Rupert, who lives in fear of earthquakes and volcanoes, has some qualms about the location. He is currently in the market for some real estate—a nice, stable, tremor-and-hot-lava-free mountain that would fit a seven-year-old budget.

His journal is filled with diagrams (arrows, enlarged areas to show detail, written explanations) that he and his friends have drawn. One boy drew a village of glass houses, but that was soundly rejected by the rest of the group who saw that the idea was "clearly" impractical. (Okay, I punned again. Forgive me.) Another boy drew floating houses as an obviously more reasonable alternative. Rupert designed a large bucket for collecting rainwater with pipes leading to their inner sanctum and a pool for the water Pokemon.

It's all very cute from my perspective, but all very serious from his. This is the world he lives in. Other boys talk about being firefighters and policemen when they grow up. Not my son. When Rupert "is a dad" (a.k.a. a grownup with real muscles and an income), he and his friends are going to dig out a safe mountain, establish a colony of brave men and cartoon characters, and save the reald.

I'm telling you, we're in good hands.

Actually, all this plotting and planning and dreaming *may* save the world some day, or at least a portion of it. Maybe not with Pokemon and ninjas. But the same brain that envisions these fantastic scenarios is going to keep flying free when it is armed with more knowledge and experience and maturity. If Rupert can do all of this with mere fantasy, imagine what he will be able to do with facts! He doesn't have to live in the real world with everyone else in order to save it. He can do that from another planet.

⊞ ⊞ ⊞

While he dreams of traveling to other planets, Rupert is very protective of his creations and wants to keep them with him. We watched an I-Max theater film on the Mars explorers, and Rupert watched in amazement as the film played out and he saw the robots being built with painstaking detail. However, the movie was a total tragedy for him, as the scientists sent their robots off to a place the scientists themselves would never be able to go, and they would never see their robots again.

Rupert leaned over and whispered to me, "Mom, I'm going to build robots like that, but I'm not sending them to Mars." Another planet, another reality. It's all the same to Rupert.

⌗   ⌗   ⌗

When he was three, Rupert didn't just have invisible friends. No, he had "bad guy" friends and "ghost" friends. At first, I was concerned about his choice of friends, but then I realized that it was a protective measure. Rupert, who really can envision ghosts and bad guys under his bed or in his closet, chose to deal with his fears at that stage in his life by making friends with his enemies. If he was their friend, maybe they wouldn't hurt him. And they didn't.

They did play a lot of games with him, like "Duck, Duck, Goose." He and his imaginary friends would all sit down in a circle in the middle of the living room, and Rupert would watch in suspense as one of his invisible bad guy or ghost friends would walk around the outside of the circle and tap each member on his or her invisible head. Inevitably, Rupert would be the one chosen. He would hop up, run around the outside of the circle as fast as he could, and chase down his opponent. On the times when he didn't outrun his friend, he let out an audible sigh. Oh well, better luck next time, Rupert.

You know, it was all so real to him that I almost believed it myself. It's okay; I'm not crazy. I knew there weren't *real* invisible friends involved. But to watch Rupert, it seemed so real to him that I found myself caught up in the suspense. Would he win this time? It wouldn't have taken much of my own imagination to visualize actual bad guys and ghosts sitting on my living room floor, eagerly waiting for their turns. Perhaps Bad Bart would be sitting there next to the Sundance Kid or Casper the Friendly Ghost, with remnants of oatmeal-raisin cookies in the corners of their lips and Kool-Aid mustaches.

When Rupert played "Go Fish" with his ghost friends, he would get resentful that they might be letting him win on purpose. It's no fun when someone lets you win. Never mind the fact that he was looking at their cards and playing for them.

⊞　⊞　⊞

Everything is an adventure for Rupert. One morning at breakfast, he dreamed out loud, "Mom, don't you think it would be cool if a bunch of jets flew over our house and men jumped out with their parachutes and said, 'Our boss wants us to be your servants. How can we help you build your ship?'"

Recently, Rupert woke up and lifted his shirt to show Pandora his spider bite. Pandora said, "Holy cow, you're covered with spider bites, Rupert. I think you have chicken pox!"

Sure enough.

We tried to convince him that they were radioactive spider bites and that he was going to be a hundred times more powerful than Spiderman. We suggested that he call himself "Arachno Guy" and told him he ought to design a costume for himself so he could keep his real identity secret.

Rupert asked me, "Mom, is that true?" He had his doubts; yet at the same time, he had a hopeful smile on his face. He wanted it to be true, even though he knew it probably wasn't.

I said, "Well, Rupert, what do you think?"

"I think it isn't true."

"You're right."

"Oh. Darn it."

It may not be true, and Rupert may be fully aware of that, but I can pretty much guarantee you that Rupert went to bed that night dreaming of being a superhero. Even an illness can be fodder for the imagination.

Rupert, like many children with hyperactive imaginations, has a secret door in his brain that will take him anywhere he wants to go. This talent does not always serve him well in school, but hey, first grade isn't everything. It's just the foundation for his education. It's just the place where he firms up his reading skills and math basics. Oh well.

🏱 🏱 🏱

I remember when I was in second grade and the world of reading was fully opened to me. Books were my ticket to another life—something more exciting than recess and my second-grade woes. I had a hyperactive imagination as it was, but those books fed my dreams with ever-new ideas.

Much like my now pre-teen daughter Pandora, I used to hide a book in my bed most nights and read in the dark, even though my mom had explained that it would ruin my eyes. During second grade, my favorite books were the *Little House on the Prairie* series by Laura Ingalls Wilder. I wanted to live in Laura's world. I began to make plans for my future. I would live in an old log cabin and weave my own straw hats and color my butter with carrot squeezings like they did in her books.

As I grew older, this dream never went away; though it did alter some. My dream log cabin home changed to a Queen Anne style, thanks to some gothic mysteries I read as I grew older. When I was a teen, I used to envision a house without any contemporary pieces, and above all, no plastic. I wanted a cow and a garden. I was iffy about electricity. I dreamed of wearing my hair up in a Gibson Girl pompadour and wearing high-neck lacy collars. These are pretty weird dreams for an all-American teenage girl.

Since those teen years, reality has set in. I think it might have had something to do with having children. I certainly don't have time for a cow, and although I love my garden, it's a luxury, because I don't have time for it, either. High-neck lacy collars? Are you kidding? T-shirts are far more practical. And heavens to Betsy, what would I do without Tupperware and plastic sandwich bags?

But somewhere, hiding in a treasure chest in my brain, those old dreams still exist. Every once in a while, they sneak out to tease me, and I feel a sudden urge to buy a cow and some chickens. Maybe a goat, for a little goat milk and cheese.

Living in the real world isn't all it's cracked up to be. It's full of bills and stress and unpleasant people who live next door or work in the next cubicle. It's full of Brussels sprouts and earthworms. I remind myself that those cows would need to be milked every morning and every night. Do I really want to commit myself to that? No, I don't. Going to the store for milk is a lot easier.

🔳 🔳 🔳

The real world is everywhere. As Fritzie said to her mother, "I want to live in the jungle so no one can find us." She gestured out the window to prove her point. "See? There are houses over there."

We must spend a little time in the real world every day if we want to earn a living or drive safely on the freeway, or go to school, for that matter. But it's okay to occasionally let the mind wander to explore new or usual ideas and thoughts. It's okay to be optimistic. It's okay to dream.

Recently, when Stanley and his friend Cranston were talking about starting their own independent film production company, they began to envision what success might look like. Cranston said, "You know, Stanley, we'd better find girlfriends now, because later, they'll just want us for our money."

Stanley shrugged his shoulders and replied, "Hey, whatever works. I can live with that."

They were both practical and still dreaming—each in his own way.

🔳 🔳 🔳

Dreaming, or imagining, is like taking a mental vacation. You already know how it feels to be in the middle of winter cold and grayness and scraping snow off the car. You know what it's like to want to take your body someplace warm and sunny where you can sip a cool drink and be grateful for it. Our brains yearn for the same kinds of escapes, only brain travel is much cheaper and you don't have to make reservations. You may want to be choosy about when and where, but other than that, it's pretty convenient.

We create our own worlds by traveling in our mind, by imagining. We also create our own worlds in reality, when we are in safe places where we are free to be ourselves.

I like living in this world we have created as a rather unusual family. I love watching Rupert create "realds" of his own design. Yes, my mother is a little eccentric, and I'm afraid all of us children have inherited that to one extreme or another, but eccentric is the opposite of boring. When I get up in the morning, I never know what the day will bring. Oh sure, the sun will come up, and the sun will go down. Bills and junk mail will fill my mailbox. There will be dishes to wash and toilets to scrub, and the price of gasoline will go up again. I will have meetings and people to deal with. But I know that I have my own sanctuary to return to. At the end of the day, I will have experienced Magnolia's cooking experiments gone awry, Otto's newest line of duct tape fashion—footwear, headgear, and jewelry (he recently made a cool-looking ring for one of his female college friends), Stanley's bizarre sense of humor, Pandora's artwork, or Rupert's flights of fancy.

You know what? I'll take my world any day.

7: A Little Intensity Goes a Long Way

When I was younger, my friends and I used to go to the roller rink and race around the arena, hoping to impress some of the cute guys enough that they would come ask us to be partners for the couples' skate. I rarely got asked to skate during the couples' skate. Later, I realized that it might have had something to do with the boys valuing their own lives enough to stay out of my way on the rink. I was a deadly hazard. If I didn't injure myself, I was bound to injure the person closest to me. Oh, I could pick up a pretty good pace, but it involved the flailing of my limbs and also the possibility of breaking bones. What was worse, once I got going, I didn't know how to stop. My only option was to run into a wall—always with the hope that nobody else was standing in between me and that wall.

I ride a bike the same way. I don't know how to use the hand brakes.

My sister Edna has the same problem with skis. She usually looks for a van or a tree that she can use as a stopping wall.

Thankfully, both Edna and I *have* by now learned how to use the brakes on our automotive vehicles. It's nice to build up speed, but if you can't control it, you can't really use it properly.

The same is true of speeding brains and their intensity. Drivers and operators should use caution.

Intensity is what happens when super determination or a super passion matches up with a speeding brain. It's par for the course in the average gifted personality—even though there is really no such thing as an average gifted personality.

❖ ❖ ❖

Intensity can affect the senses. Pandora, who loves music and takes piano lessons, tells me that she can hear music playing in her ears—not imagine it playing or pretend like it's playing or recall hearing it played. No. None of that. She can actually hear it in her ears.

It happened the first time when we were riding home from school one day. Pandora made an announcement. "Mom, I can hear music, just like it's playing. I can hear music in my ears. It's the most awesome thing that has ever happened to me!"

She even went so far as to say she didn't think she needed a CD player anymore. This is quite a declaration, since she loves her CD player, but it seems that her brain has begun to take over the job.

She said she had been imagining in her mind that she was playing the music to *The Phantom of the Opera* on the piano and going over the fingering. (*Phantom* is my children's all-time favorite music. The other day, Rupert was even singing to the tune of the "Angel of Music" the words, "I have to go-oh po-o-o-otteeee!") As Pandora was playing the notes in her mind, she began hearing the music from the CD with all of the instruments.

I assumed she was imagining the music, but she said no, she didn't hear it in her mind; she could actually hear it in her ears, and it was louder in one ear than in the other. She couldn't hear the entire song, but just certain sections of it, and only the music, not the voices. (Thank goodness for that. I don't mind if my daughter hears music, but I'd really prefer she didn't hear voices. Not unless they're telling her to clean her room or be nice to her mother.)

She tried to make it happen again, but she couldn't do it when we were talking. And then we hit the bumpy dirt road, and she said that was a distraction, too. But she knows she can do it.

My three youngest children love *The Phantom of the Opera* in an intense way. Magnolia decided to try taking piano lessons and stuck with them long enough to learn how to play songs from the musical. Rupert was initially fascinated with the whole idea of a "vampire" of the opera, but once he found the music, that was it. He was truly smitten. For a while, everything he wanted to say he said to the tune of *Phantom* music.

I thought it was just us, but when we had a carpet-layer working on the stairs in our entryway, lo and behold, the carpet-layer hummed away at the *Phantom* theme. A kindred spirit!

▦   ▦   ▦

Of course, having a carpet-layer in our home was just one more new and interesting experience for Rupert. The man was kind enough to give Rupert some scraps.

Rupert thinks carpet scraps are even cooler than piles of dirt or rocks. He wanted to bring the scraps to school for show and tell. Magnolia, mortified, tried to talk him out of it, but Stanley, the guy who once brought a fabric softener sheet and a rubber band to school for show and tell when he was in first grade, was all for sharing carpet scraps in the classroom.

A week later, Rupert was still walking around with his precious scraps rolled up neatly and carried under one arm. At night, when I checked on him, I often found carpet scraps laying on the floor, all lined up to look like a rug. When we went somewhere, I had to ask him to leave the carpet scraps at home, please. Thankfully, they were a little too bulky for him to stuff into his pants pockets.

I eventually put my foot down, because we simply do not have enough room in our house to keep everything that this kid wants to collect and save. I limited Rupert to one piece of carpet, so he chose his favorite scrap. That was over a year ago. He still has it.

Rupert develops an intense attachment to things for reasons I can't always comprehend. When my mom gave him an old wooden miniature tiki (a Polynesian carved statue of a human form), he was in seventh heaven. He didn't play with it; he just refused to part with it under any circumstances. I sat next to him in church one day and noticed the wooden head of the tiki poking out of his slacks' pocket.

When we went on an overnight trip for spring break this year, headed for a nice hotel, seven-year-old Rupert packed all of his necessities in plain brown bags. I have a "don't ask, don't tell" policy, at least at those times when I really would rather not know, or when I am too much in a hurry to get out the door or too tired to argue. Rupert toted his bags in the wastebasket from his bedroom (he was bringing his wastebasket just in case the hotel room didn't have one, he said). After we got to our hotel, I noticed that the mysterious contents had found their way to a corner of our room. Rupert had brought various paper scraps, a plastic cup with two holes punched near the top on both sides, and his tiki. I can only assume he had some kid ritual in mind, because these weren't typical play toys—except for maybe a kid like Rupert. When he likes something, he *really* likes it.

⊞   ⊞   ⊞

Intense people don't just enjoy things, they become *enamored*. They take their relationships with objects, with ideas, or with hobbies to the next level. They develop passions. These passions do not always turn into long-term relationships, but many do—like the passion my 21-year-old son Stanley has had for the movie industry for the last 19 years. Or the passion my mom has for studying animals, bugs, and science experiments. My daughter Magnolia, however, has yet to develop her lasting love. She experiences passionate flings with various ideas, people, and objects. When she loves something, that something is the ultimate and all-powerful force in her life. But when it's over, it's over. She's like a bee flitting from flower to flower. "Oh, here's a good one! What nectar! How divine! I've discovered the source of ultimate happiness!" Then, after a day or so, it's, "Okay, that's enough. Next."

The key is not necessarily time or duration—it's the intensity.

🃏 🃏 🃏

One of my friends is a firefighter. He loves everything about his job. He loves it with a passion. He subscribes to firefighter magazines. He listens to his radio at all hours, just in case. He collects models of fire trucks. He buys them for his wife and children, too, because if he loves fire trucks that much, well then, how could others not get as excited about them or think they're as cool as he does? Firefighting is not just his career—it's his life. It's who he is.

I have another friend who gets really excited about political topics. I get excited about politics as well, but only in my spare time. (Spare time? As if.) It doesn't matter, because this friend is constantly researching particular topics and e-mailing me the results. This is great; he's doing the work for me, and I find the results interesting. But I am not passionate enough to invest large amounts of time hunting down the clues. He is. He's spent months now on the same topic, and he has yet to run out of steam.

My sister Hortense is passionate about housecleaning. Go figure. I have no idea where this passion came from; it isn't genetic—no one else in the family has been afflicted in the same way. But you can show up at my sister's house anytime, day or night, and it will look as though it has just been vacuumed and smell as though it has just been dusted with lemon-scented furniture polish. She washes her pillowcases every day. Every day, mind you! We enjoy going to her house, because it feels good—like walking into, oh, I don't know, a really clean house. And I think it's good for my kids to know what a really clean house looks like, just in case they ever decide they would like to pursue the same course. (Keep your fingers crossed for me.)

Hortense has trained her children to be fastidious as well. When her young daughter comes to my house, if she sees something on the floor, she will pick it up and bring it to me with a look of disappointment. I think even Hortense's dog is trained to lick up specks of dust that the vacuum may have missed. Hortense loves having a clean house, and she loves the time she spends cleaning. Her yard is just as immaculate. Housework or mowing the lawn may be drudgery for some, but for her, it is intensely pleasurable. I keep reminding her that she is free to take on my house, too, at any time, but only because I love her. I would hate to have her run out of things to do.

⊞　　⊞　　⊞

Intense-brain people often develop, or desire to develop, intense relationships with friends or lovers. They are usually not half-way devotees, but put their whole hearts into their relationships, unless they are otherwise distracted by all-encompassing passions for other interests that leave no room for relationships. It is difficult for some gifted people to find friends and lovers who understand their needs and are willing and able to meet them. This can lead to feelings of loneliness and isolation, even while they are surrounded by many people who do care for them and love them. Their intensity may push some prospective friends away—perhaps even people who could have been friends if they hadn't been so overwhelmed by the natural intensity of the gifted person.

When gifted people, at any age, fall in love or look for a best friend and confidant, they may immediately invest more emotion and commitment to the relationship than the other person is ready to reciprocate. They may long for a true companion with whom they can share their deepest feelings and thoughts. They want to be understood and loved, and yet it is a rarity for them to find another person who can give and take with the intensity and understanding longed for by the passionate gifted heart.

When Rupert was in kindergarten, he made friends with a very bright and intense boy name Garrett who called pretty much every day and often invited himself over. If Rupert wasn't around to talk, Garrett was okay with that. He didn't mind having a conversation with me. I was a little taken back by the demanding and confident voice of the five-year-old on the other end of the line.

"So what are you doing right now?" he would ask.

"I'm just taking care of a few things," I said, hoping that he would think me boring and hang up the phone so I really could take care of a few things.

"Huh. How old are you anyway?"

"Older than you."

"Yeah, but *how* old?"

"You know, Garrett, I really need to get back to work."

"Okay, but when can I come over? My mom said you could pick me up from school tomorrow."

I have no doubt she did.

Then, an intense little girl, Geraldine, began calling Rupert when he went to first grade. She wasn't insistent on getting to know the person on the other end of the phone unless it was Rupert. Even then, she was more interested in sharing her information than she was in listening to anyone else's. She called at least once a day for a week or so. Once, when Stanley answered the phone, he hung up, laughing.

"What's so funny?" I asked.

"That was Geraldine. She was asking for Rupert, but I heard her mom yelling in the background, 'Are you on the phone again? I thought I told you to stop!'"

Later that evening, Geraldine managed to sneak in another shot at a conversation. She called for Rupert and told him, "My parents told me I can't talk on the phone anymore, because I keep telling everyone their secrets."

These are young gifted brains just starting out on the rocky road of relationships. However, adult relationships are not so different.

It is important for those who are intense brains to learn to recognize the needs of others involved in their relationships. Some friends cannot handle the demands or may need some time to get used to the intensity rather than getting hit in the face with it all at once. If little Geraldine loves everything to do with birds and can recognize and name every local species as well as their bird calls, that's terrific. That makes her a more interesting person. However, when she invites her new friend Sally over to play, she may want to avoid enthusiastically bombarding Sally with hundreds of tidbits and facts and her entire bird collection all at once. Faced with such intensity, some unsuspecting potential friends might get out of there as fast as they can. Sometimes the intense brain must learn to temper itself. If Geraldine can learn to share her passion with her new friend in smaller doses, she might actually whet Sally's appetite for more.

For example, if they are sitting out on the back doorstep eating popsicles and a bird sings out, Geraldine could casually say, "There goes the yellow-bellied sapsucker." To which Sally might ask, "What? How do you know?" Geraldine could shrug her shoulders and say, "Hear that one in the tree over there? That's a robin. She's got babies to feed right now," which would likely inspire more questions from Sally. If Geraldine is careful not to feed Sally any more than she asks for, Geraldine may soon find that Sally's interest has grown to a point where Geraldine can share her bird passion with an eager and sympathetic ear.

Intense brains need to realize that, while they may need to adjust to other people's needs and temper their intensity in certain situations, intensity itself is not always a bad thing, and there are some people out there who will readily understand and relate. Over the years, I have found myself telling each of my children, when they get to about fifth or sixth grade and are feeling lonely and isolated, that they *will* find a best friend some day. Best friends are rare gifts, but they do happen. Until then, work with what you have and get involved in activities that you are intensely passionate about. Chances are you may meet someone else as enthusiastic and intense as you are.

As for myself, out of the hundreds of good people I have associated with, I can count on one hand the people I believe really understand me. I have learned that that's okay. I know I'm not alone. There *are* others like me. I look forward to meeting them.

⊞　⊞　⊞

There are so many things to be intense about. Gifted kids, and adults, often want to learn with an intense yearning. Unfortunately, the typical classroom often won't provide enough for the really quick and intense brains, so eager for information. When my mom Myrna was in second grade, she ate up the section on dinosaurs, and just when she was really getting into it and wanted to learn everything there is to know about dinosaurs, the section was over. The chapter on dinosaurs was just a teaser.

A lot of rapid-learning kids like Myrna feel ripped off. They aren't satisfied with the basic introductory info that most textbooks offer. They would like to cram a whole lot more depth into their school year.

This is one reason I have a library at home. My husband tells me that if I buy one more book, our house will fall over. I'm not too worried about it, though, since we don't have any neighbors on the hillside immediately below. But I wonder if our homeowner's insurance covers book overload. What can I say? I have an intense passion for books.

"Intensity" could be used to describe every characteristic of giftedness. It is as though the brain is running ahead, working overtime, and can't let go. You've heard the phrase, "Anything worth doing is worth doing well." The fast brain does not know any other rule, except for the rule that says, "If it's not worth doing well, it's not worth doing at all, and so why am I wasting my time with this trivial and meaningless task when I could be doing something worth doing?" Which explains why some very bright minds seem to underachieve in school. It just isn't worth the effort to them.

It probably also explains the pile of dishes in my sink. A person only has so much time and so much energy to invest.

The other side of the intensity coin means that those tasks, people, and objects that do not demand or earn the full attention of the rapid brain will fall away somewhere along the wayside, neglected and forgotten, like the crusts of a peanut butter and jelly sandwich after a four-year-old has finished devouring the tasty middle.

Intensity can be a positive and productive thing, but it must also be managed. It's like a power tool. You wouldn't use a chainsaw to cut up your steak, but then, a steak knife would be totally useless if you needed to cut some firewood.

⌗ ⌗ ⌗

Coping with intensity means that one must learn to size up the situation and decide which tool is needed for the job. Sometimes the best thing to do is let intensity run free and wild, as a brain explores all of the incredible possibilities in the surrounding world. Other times it's best to set that intensity aside for a few minutes and work on something else—like remembering to put gas in the car or pay the electric bill.

Dang. I hate it when that happens. There are too many trivial and mundane necessities of life that get in my way. I have feelings to vent! I have books to write! I have paintings to paint! I have projects to create! I am intensity, mixed with creativity. Hear me roar!

But first, I have a few dishes to wash.

8: Living with Good Intentions

I recently heard about a little boy who said to his dad, "When I grow up, I'm going to be a mommy." He just wanted to follow family tradition and be like his five older sisters. As near as he could tell, all of the kids in the family were going to grow up to be mommies. He figured that was a given for him, too. He meant well. It made sense at the time.

When my sister Gertrude and I get together, our brains go nuts bouncing off each other. We come up with all kinds of brilliant ideas and plans. We have books to write together and businesses to start. How many of those plans have we carried out? Honestly, not one. But we do have a great time thinking and scheming and laughing together. And we do intend to do something about at least *some* of our plans someday. Someday.

So many times we want to do the right things, but other things pop up. I think we should get some points for at least having good intentions. Maybe a half-point. I don't know.

Sometimes we get side-tracked because we are human, and even though we start off heading in the right direction, a more tempting proposition comes along. Other times we intend to do well, but our quick brain gets in the way.

I'll give you an example of the first. On Valentine's Day, my dad Harold always bought my mom Myrna a big, heart-shaped box of chocolates. He meant well. He wanted to do something special for her, but as he was browsing the aisles, a little voice popped into his head.

"Harold, did you see the chocolate?"

"Yes, I love chocolate. That's what *I* would like for Valentine's Day."

"Well, if you buy some for Myrna, I'll bet she would share some with you, and that's what relationships are all about, right? Sharing things together?"

"Remember, Myrna is on a diet. She doesn't want chocolate for Valentine's Day."

"Tsk, tsk, tsk, Harold. Why is Myrna on a diet? Because she likes candy. She likes chocolate. Get her what she likes, Harold. You can help her out with her diet by eating some of it yourself. And isn't that what marriage is all about? Helping each other through the tough times?"

"But...."

"It's a pretty box, Harold. And it's big. Show her how much you love her, Harold. And I'll bet there are some chocolate-covered cherries in that box, too. Your fa-a-a-avorite."

"Well," Harold says with a sigh, "I don't really know what else to get her. A large box of chocolates with some potential cherry cordials would be better than coming home empty-handed."

"That's right, Harold."

"Okay. I'll do it!"

My mom received many boxes of chocolates throughout the years—though I think in the later years, Harold's conscience began to get the better of him. And now that our family owns a chocolate shop, it has become almost (*almost!*) ridiculous to buy chocolates, even for my dad.

During all those years, those heart-shaped boxes were intended to say, "I love you. Can I have some? Are you going to eat that caramel?" Harold had good intentions, but his taste buds stepped in and sabotaged his plans.

⌗ ⌗ ⌗

When you're gifted, your brain sometimes does the same thing—just like the fourth grader who intends to follow along with the rest of the class during a read-aloud session with the science textbook, but when his eyes get to the words "force" and "acceleration," his brain runs off without any warning and without any permission and takes him to a galaxy far, far away, where Luke Skywalker is zooming in to destroy the Death Star. Let's say this fourth grader has a name, and his name is Zues. This is the conversation in Zues's head between his brain and his conscience.

Brain: "Yikes! This is miserable. I can't focus on each word at such a slow rate. I want to zoom! I want to explore!"

Conscience: "I'm afraid we can't do that, Brain. We have been told countless numbers of times that we must stay with the rest of the class. We have promised the teacher that we will do better."

Brain: "But we are already 18 paragraphs ahead!"

Conscience: "Yes, and thank goodness we can't turn the page, or we would be even more off track. At least we are on the same *page* as everyone else this time. The teacher gets frustrated when we turn pages at the wrong moments. It disrupts the rest of the class and proves that we are not conforming and being obedient."

Brain: "I can't sit still this long!"

Conscience: "No, I am determined that this time we are going to do it. This time we *will* follow along. We will *not* be distracted."

Brain: "Hey, did you hear that?"

Conscience: "Hear what?"

Brain: "Ha! Caught you! You weren't listening because you were talking to me."

Conscience: "Oh great. I knew you were going to mess me up. What did I miss? Where are we? The teacher could call on us at any moment to read, and she will be so disappointed with us if we are lost!"

Brain: "Remember that part about force? You know, 16 paragraphs ago?"

Conscience: "Yeah, that was pretty interesting."

Brain: "Well heck yeah, force is interesting. Remember that movie we saw with that tall guy who breathes through a mask?"

Conscience: "Oh yeah, you mean Darth Vader!"

Brain: "Yeah, and that Luke kid. He used the Force, remember? That was *so* cool!"

Conscience: "Wait a minute! I know what you're doing. You're trying to distract me so you can follow your own train of thought. I'm here to see that doesn't happen. No sirree, you're not going to get past me this time. Okay, where are we now?"

Brain: "The girl two seats in front of you just finished reading about acceleration. Acceleration. That's all about speed you know."

Conscience: "Oh hey, I remember reading about that."

Brain: "I wonder how fast Luke Skywalker was going when he was trying to maneuver his way through that narrow gap to hit the target that would destroy the Death Star."

Conscience: "He had to be going hundreds of miles an hour or something. And the whole time, he was relying on that Force thingy."

Brain: "I wonder how the Force works? Does it control his mind? Does it guide his hands?"

Teacher: "Zues? Zues? It's your turn to read. You promised me you would stay with the class this time."

Conscience: "Curses, foiled again!"

"What page are we on again, please?"

The brain has this extreme desire to pursue its own course at its own rate of speed. It does not heed gravity. It does not necessarily heed convention. It flashes, and that flash ignites another flash, and another flash, and so on, until the brain has traveled an unpredictable path and ended up where it may not have intended to go. Yes, the brain can be controlled. We can choose to think or to not think about certain things. But there is a natural desire to pursue thoughts to their ends. This is a good thing as long as we can manage it, channel it, and re-channel it when needed.

❖ ❖ ❖

Keeping your brain on track requires self-discipline, which is a hard-earned skill, and most children and teens are only in the beginning stages of learning the process and developing the will to do so. Even as adults, few of us can say that we have completely mastered the art of self-discipline. Being intellectually or creatively gifted may imply that brains are running at a faster rate of speed or in unique and interesting directions, but it does not automatically mean that fast brains are self-disciplined. Gifted people still get distracted—perhaps even more than the general population. They make mistakes. They have good intentions, but their brains run off with their judgment or their self-discipline. The fact is, smart people are perfectly capable of doing stupid things.

Stanley is a really smart kid, but you'd never know it by looking at any of his cars—and he's now on his third! He rolled the first car two months after he got his driver's license. Was he speeding or showing off? Nope. Nothing like that. He was simply traveling down our own little dirt road at about 20 miles an hour. His brain went wandering off somewhere and left his car on automatic pilot. He thought he was safe on that empty dirt road, but before he knew it, he found himself drifting off the side of the road and up the hillside, and then before he knew it, both he and the car were upside down. The good news is that he didn't get seriously injured, and he didn't seriously injure anyone else. (Looking on the bright side.) Thankfully, he learned his lesson (pay attention when driving) in a safe and traffic-free environment. The car looked like a tin can that had been stepped on, but it still worked. After Hubby crawled inside, pushed the top back up with his feet, and replaced the front windshield, Stanley was able to drive it to school until he graduated. Forget the gaps where the passenger side door didn't quite meet with the rest of the car. And he didn't mind the funny looks when people saw his car, because Stanley likes to be different. His car might as well be different, too.

The second car lasted longer—until last year when he first ran out of gas, later missed a curve, and then blew out his engine because he forgot to check the oil and put some in now and then—and all this within a two-week period. Mechanical things are not Stanley's forte. Now, with his third car, Stanley has every intention of making sure the oil is changed. He's learning as he goes—in increments. In his case, experience seems to be the best (maybe the only?) teacher.

※ ※ ※

As for me, I am not much better. I get distracted easily, too.

When we first moved into our present home, I was excited to have people over. I planned a huge dinner and invited family and friends. I decided that to feed a large number of people in style and on a budget, I would take a turkey from our freezer and make all the fixin's to go with it. I made pumpkin pies, rolls, mashed potatoes, fruit salad, stuffing, and I even opened a can or two of cranberry sauce. My husband was thrilled, because he loves a good meal, as do I, but I usually have a tendency to avoid the kitchen unless I'm hungry and I want a quick snack. A turkey dinner that involves so many side dishes usually means leftovers for days, so I was pretty happy about this whole thing, for my own selfish reasons, too. My mind conjured up images of impressed and satisfied guests and alternated to those images of microwaveable leftovers. It was going to be a win-win situation for everyone.

About an hour before the company was due to arrive, my husband asked, "Did you remember to put the turkey in the oven?"

Dang. I knew I was forgetting something.

I quickly whipped up a large batch of spaghetti, which we ate with mashed potatoes (no gravy without a turkey), cranberry sauce, and stuffing.

You know what? I began with good intentions. It was all that imagining of the results that got in my way. My brain took off on other projects without finishing the one that it started, which turned out to be the most important one—the main course. Fortunately, my family understands and accepts me, and everyone had a good laugh. And the other good news is that I haven't forgotten to put a turkey in the oven since.

I have discovered in my life that I am doubly blessed. Not only do I trip over my own feet, but I stumble over my own feats, as well.

⊞   ⊞   ⊞

When we use the term "absent-minded," it means that the brain has hung out a sign on its door that says, "Gone to pursue other interests. Will be back shortly." It doesn't mean that the brain isn't working; it's just not working on what it's "supposed" to be working on. Sometimes those other interests are more worthy of thought than the original task. Sometimes not.

When Magnolia was about seven, she won a pair of goldfish at a carnival, and she was thrilled. She couldn't wait to get them home and to set them up with a place of their own. She had every intention of providing them with a good life. We found a fish bowl and set it up with an old aerator pump—we didn't know if they needed aeration, but we thought it would be better to be safe than sorry. Magnolia proudly displayed the fish on the top of her dresser. And then she moved on to other things. It took me a week to get suspicious that the poor creatures might have entered the next life and gone on to pursue more spiritual prospects. It took me so long because the pump kept moving the water around, and the fish looked as though they were still swimming. As for Magnolia, she hadn't noticed a thing. Her brain had been excited about the fish for one or two days, and then it had moved on, distracted by other things. Her brain has a tendency to say "Oh, cool!" in about 10 different directions at once before it moves immediately on to 10 other exciting ideas.

When she was 13 and wanted a dog, I envisioned those fish and nearly said no. However, we decided to give her a chance, and this time it was a different story. The dog was more than exciting, it was interesting in a deeper way, and Magnolia was able to follow through with her good intentions. It held her interest *and* her emotions. It lasted *beyond* her intentions.

⊞　⊞　⊞

My husband has his embarrassing moments, too. It's absent-mindedness that gets him into trouble. It's probably not wise to habitually leave your checkbook on the register counter after your latest purchase. In his case, he is so worried about calculating and tallying the numbers in his bank account that after he writes the check, he forgets to pick up the tool that makes it all possible. His brain is always someplace else—usually on the next task—and it sometimes leaves him short of help in whatever his current situation may be. His brain does not follow along or stay with his body. It reads ahead.

He is used to this, though he does find it frustrating. Most of the situations are manageable, and we are grateful for the fact that we live in a small town and many a store clerk has called us to let us know that he or she has my husband's checkbook. He intends to never forget it again, but the only way that will really happen is if it is permanently attached to his wrist by a short bungee cord. His brain is just way too busy to be bothered with trivial details like remembering everyday items. He won't use a debit card, because his brain insists on a written record, and it loves immediately tallying those numbers in his checkbook.

⊞　⊞　⊞

As part of his job, my husband occasionally works at a lab where he repairs equipment. The lab is at the highest security level. He has to go through a long process just to get in the door. One day, he was in the middle of a job when he realized that he had forgotten a necessary tool in his car. So he left his bag of tools near the equipment and went out to fetch the tool he needed. While he was rummaging around in the toolbox, he received a call on his cell phone. It was my dad Harold, who is also my husband's boss.

My husband answered the phone. "Hello?"

Harold asked, "Where are you at?"

"The lab. Why? Actually, I'm in the car at the moment, but I'm going back in."

"You didn't happen to leave your tool bag inside, did you?"

"Yes."

"Well, you might want to hurry in there. Someone saw the bag sitting unattended by the equipment, and they're treating it as if it's a bomb, just in case. They called me to check with you, just to make sure it wasn't something you left behind."

So my husband, who doesn't like to call attention to himself, had to go through the long process of re-entering the building and then make his way through the crowd to let them know that the bag that they suspected might be a bomb was just his tool bag he had left behind.

⊞   ⊞   ⊞

He always has the best of intentions, and one of his biggest intentions is to do everything well, or at least correctly. He hates mistakes, especially his own. He's a perfectionist. (Sigh.) Perfectionists struggle the most with their intentions, because their unrealistically high intentions rarely meet up with their actual human performance. By the way, you'll know if you're a perfectionist. If you are unsure, ask the people around you. They'll know.

Pandora and Otto are both perfectionists in some ways. They want to do things properly—or make sure other people are doing things properly. Rules are important to them. They are both constantly checking my speedometer to make sure I am complying with the laws of the land. And Pandora, who hates to be late and in fact would like to be about 20 minutes *early*, will want me to obey the speed limit signs even if it means she won't be on time. Apparently, she has a hierarchy of rules.

I am worried that I might be developing a perfectionist child. This is not an entirely bad thing, but I hope my 10-year-old Pandora can keep a sense of balance in her life.

Pandora is in fourth grade. She studies. She completes every extra credit assignment and then asks for more. She keeps saying that she doesn't want an A+, she wants an A+++++. After raising a few less-than-motivated scholars, this comes as a blessed relief to my grateful mommy heart and my own disorganized brain, as I have never been gifted at organizational skills like keeping track of homework and due dates. I feel a great burden lifted knowing that Pandora will keep track of her own assignments and get them done on time and done well. I hope she continues her dedication to her academic pursuits. I hope she strives for high standards in all of the important areas of her life. I hope she meets challenges with delightful anticipation rather than a shirking shrug of her shoulders.

And I hope that she can do all of this without feeling as though she is a failure if she doesn't reach every goal.

The other day, she built a diorama of the inside of a Norwegian house on a snowy day to go along with a book they were reading in class. She did a terrific job. She used a box with a hinged lid that would open to reveal the scene, which included a backdrop she had carefully drawn on the back of the box. She built a table and bench out of popsicle sticks. She modeled dishes and food out of clay. She's a pretty darn good artist (she seems to be a pretty darn good everything—which goes along with that "A+ isn't good enough" attitude). Anyway, she showed it to me. I was suitably impressed. She asked me if there was anything I would have done differently.

That's when the creative side of me pushed the mommy side of me out of the way. I love miniature stuff. So I said, "Well, if you had more time, you could have made real curtains out of fabric, and you could have cut a thick piece of fabric out for a rug, and molded little boots out of clay to place beside the door instead of drawing them there.…" I was thinking, "Hey, this could be a real fun project."

Pandora agreed with me.

Later, she said she got an A- on her project. She told me that she was supposed to grade herself, and she gave herself a C- because she really *should* have done *everything* in 3-D. The scene could have been so much better.

That's when her teacher said, "No, honey. You're being too hard on yourself. Let's give it an A-."

When Pandora told me this, I thought, "Ack! What am I doing to my child? I'm driving her to extreme perfection! I didn't mean to, really!"

It was a small thing, I know. But it illustrated to me that my kids sometimes take what I say more seriously than I intend. How many times have I unintentionally implied that good enough wasn't really good enough, and Pandora, or one of my other children, hasn't said anything and just carried the weight of believing that he or she was coming up short?

It is difficult to maintain a balance myself. I want my children to aim high, but I have to be careful to acknowledge when certain efforts are high enough. I've got to push (I mean encourage) them to reach their potential and yet recognize when to pull back and let things slide.

⊞   ⊞   ⊞

One of the things Pandora has discovered is that she needs to work on her tendency to procrastinate. She wants to do things well, but when she learned what the word "procrastinate" meant, she realized that doing things well would be much easier if she didn't wait until the last minute. She went madly to work on a castle scene—which for her means an entire castle with two towers that have cut-away walls to display the rooms inside, a great hall, and a working drawbridge. And that was just the beginning. Keep in mind that this project hadn't even been assigned yet. Her teacher just happened to mention that she planned to assign a castle diorama in the spring.

Pandora doesn't want to procrastinate. She wants to be perfect. She has the best of intentions, but where are those intentions going to take her? If she can learn to manage them, they may help her to pursue and accomplish great things in the directions of her passions. If she doesn't learn to manage them, she could end up getting treatment for ulcers.

⊞ ⊞ ⊞

Sometimes our intentions themselves take us down the wrong path. We mean well, but we really don't have enough understanding of the situation to make a better choice—or we refuse to consider that there may be other options because we've already become attached to a self-preferred "best" option.

When Magnolia was born, I was so excited to have a girl—not because I didn't appreciate boys, but because I wanted to give a daughter all of the things I had wanted when I was growing up. I waited with great patience for her third Christmas, when I could finally move beyond baby and toddler toys and get to the gold standard of girly-stuff—Barbie dolls. I loved Barbies when I was a kid. I made clothes for them. I stacked boxes to make houses for them. I even kept a doll alive in my mind as she lived in the house I made for her on the shelves of my headboard. I brought her real food. I made her a soft bed out of socks and a washcloth. You get the idea. I loved dolls, but especially Barbies. When Magnolia was three, I wanted to give her all of those wonderful things I could only have in my imagination, and so I started with the biggest item of all—a huge, sturdy, beautiful, pink dollhouse, Barbie-sized.

Do you know what Magnolia did with her new Barbies? She tossed them aside. Can you believe that? She was more interested in her brothers' stuff. She liked the big pink dollhouse, but only because she could climb on it. And she discovered that if she laid down on her side, she could squeeze her entire body through the front door.

This was of course discouraging, because my dream of how she would react had been burst. Ever persistent and optimistic, I thought perhaps she hadn't yet reached the developmental maturity level necessary to appreciate the value of Barbie toys. So the next Christmas, I supplied her with a car, furniture, and even little tiny knives, forks, and spoons. Nope, she still wasn't ready. The next year, I tried again, this time with a horse and carriage set. She had to admit that the horse was pretty cool, but that's as far as she got. The toys sat unused in her room—with the exception of the dollhouse/jungle gym.

It took me a few years to realize that my little girl wasn't the same little girl that I had been. I had to quit projecting my dreams into her life. I had great intentions, but they were wrong for her. And even if they had been right for her, how fair was it to give her all of the dream stuff in the beginning and take away her opportunities to stretch her imagination? When you get the good stuff first, it's like loading up on dessert. You end up with a mental stomachache, and you don't have a whole lot to look forward to after that. But I meant well.

🏯 🏯 🏯

Sometimes good intentions are all we've got to go on, because we're short on knowledge. At these times, creativity may step in where knowledge fears to tread—or where creativity doesn't even recognize that knowledge is missing.

We see this often with songs, for example. When my sister Darleen was about 13, she used to walk around singing to the tune of "If You Love Somebody" by Sting. Originally, the words read, "If you love somebody, set them free." Darleen was unaware of this. Her version went, "If you love Tom Bosley, set him free." This left me wondering what was going on in her brain. Did she know who Tom Bosley was? Did she imagine that the father from the TV show *Happy Days* was imprisoned somewhere and there was a cultural movement to set the poor guy free? But apparently the words made sense to her. And I'm sure she felt what she said—she would have been thrilled to see Tom Bosley set free.

When Pandora was six, she walked around singing a Britney Spears song, or at least one line of it. I wasn't real excited about my young daughter emulating that particular pop star, so it gave me great pleasure to hear Pandora's innocent version using the words, "Why do these *fleas* come at night?" She hadn't picked up on the word "tears," and in her mind, "fleas" was the logical choice to fill in that blank. I did try to correct her once, but she insisted she knew what she was singing about, so I let it go. Let her wonder about the fleas. It would keep her mind busy.

We all do this to some extent. I'm willing to bet that most of us have replaced the words to a song with our own best guesses. We mean well, but sometimes we just aren't accurate. Good intentions are not enough.

🏵 🏵 🏵

Rupert, who loves to use new words and take his vocabulary out for walks, or perhaps parades, has good intentions, but sometimes he's just a tad bit off. He earned an unusually large amount of money last Christmas—unusually large for him anyway—and he wanted to spend it wisely. Since the first and most obvious place to spend money at Christmastime is on gifts for others, Rupert went shopping for gifts for his family. He carefully counted out his money each time he approached a register. After a few stores, we were at another register where he was preparing to pay for his latest purchases—again, gifts for family—and he turned to me and asked, "Mom, how much money have I wasted so far?"

The term he was looking for, I think (and hope), was "spent." But it's true that his dad has drilled into him that spending money and wasting money are practically synonymous at times if one is not careful. In Rupert's mind, the two words are interchangeable. He meant well. He had good intentions. It only *sounded* as though he considered gifts for his family as money down the drain.

🏵 🏵 🏵

Rupert has a great deal of good intentions, especially since his brain, though it may be running at a high speed, has limited experiences with life, and he relies on his creativity to fuel the brain and keep up the high rate of thinking. Remember, he plans on saving the reald someday.

Rupert has determined that he is going to lead the good guys into battle and wallop the bad guys into submission. He will then reign peacefully from his throne, Nintendo and Pokemon characters will sit at his roundtable, dragons and dinosaurs will be declared endangered and protected species, and his kindergarten flame (for whom he made a necklace last year) will sit at his side.

He is not going into this battle unprepared. He realizes that he will need strong muscles in order to heft the sword he has envisioned, so he's been working out. He lies on his back on the floor and holds a wooden chair over his head as long as his little arms will allow. My job is to time him. When he's exhausted, he retreats to the couch to regain his strength, and then back to the chair over his head. His exercise routine is rounded out with his version of kickboxing and an almost unrecognizable mutation of sit-ups.

Magnolia informed him that if he really wanted big strong muscles, he should eat his vegetables. This was not a pleasant prospect for Rupert, but he said he was willing to make the sacrifice. Then she told him that spinach was the healthiest vegetable he could eat. He asked what spinach was. (Okay, I know. Bad mom. My son had never heard of spinach before. But I figure that's what school hot lunches are for. After all, that's where *I* first tasted it.) Magnolia explained to him that spinach was a vegetable that most people didn't like. Rupert sighed and said, "Okay. I'll eat spinach, too."

There is, after all, a price to be paid for saving the reald.

He has the best of intentions. I hope that as his quick brain gains knowledge (and perhaps a little sense of reality), he'll be able to combine those good intentions with useful information and do something amazing.

Since gifted minds are often accompanied by intense passions, it's easy to get distracted by good intentions before we have all of the information necessary to bring our ultimate goals to fruition. It is easy to get in a hurry, and while creativity is an incredibly wonderful thing, it is not always a good replacement for facts. In this case, patience is a good coping skill to make sure that the ideal we intend and hope for can become a reality that we will feel good about.

On the other hand, there are times when we need to realize that good intentions are really not enough. Sometimes they are not even worth pursuing.

When my grandparents designed an adobe house, they decided to make the adobe bricks, made of straw and clay, themselves. That's how my family is—we like to create everything we can for ourselves, whenever possible, from scratch. No sense hiring somebody else to do the job when we can do it ourselves. Not unless we want it done right, anyway.

My grandparents dug a pit and filled it with clay and straw and water, and they stomped. They stomped and they stomped and they stomped. They put the mud in molds to dry. The bricks had to dry for days, weeks. They made enough bricks to do the first few layers of the walls of their home. Then they said, "This is ridiculous. Hey. I've got an idea. Let's purchase some already-made bricks!"

The house went up much more quickly after that.

I take a certain amount of pride in the fact that my grandparents tried to build their house the old-fashioned way. But at the rate they were going, it would have taken years. They would have been in great shape from all that mixing and stomping. But as far as getting the house finished, their good intentions were holding them back.

We have to decide if our good intentions are leading toward or away from productive results. And since productive results take time and patience, we may get distracted by other good intentions along the way, and we need to be aware of that, too.

114

We can cope by developing techniques to keep ourselves focused. We should press on with patience, focus, and a continual search for further information—something most hungry minds yearn for anyway.

Good intentions alone are not enough, but they are a start—especially if you want to save the reald.

9: When Science Experiments Go Bad

*O*tto's first year of college was full of memory-making moments. I think he fit classes, homework, and tests somewhere in there, too, but I'm not sure. One of his memory-making moments involved Mentos and Coke. (Mentos are a brand of mint with a reputation for causing explosions when mixed with a carbonated beverage—as seen on YouTube, *David Letterman*, and *Mythbusters*.) Otto and his dorm buddies decided to see what would happen if they mixed the two together in a sealed two-liter bottle. So being the geniuses that they are, they decided to carefully place the Mentos on several layers of tissue paper and float them in the Coke. This would give them time to seal up the bottle with duct tape before the coke soaked through the tissue and reacted with the Mentos. They wanted to see it explode in the air, so they dropped it from a six-story window.

The bottle landed with a loud bang—not because there was an explosion, but because that's what happens to two-liter plastic bottles full of liquid when they hit the ground.

Sometimes fast brains can overcome problems such as keeping the Coke and the Mentos from mixing, but then they stop short. They think things most of the way through, but most of the way may not be far enough.

The previous chapter focused on good intentions. Sometimes those good intentions fail for lack of information. Other times those good intentions bring on a whole new learning experience.

⊞　⊞　⊞

On St. Patrick's Day, Magnolia went nuts. I told her that she could color the milk green, so she colored *all* of our milk green. With our large family, we buy several gallons of milk at a time, so we had the green stuff hanging around for days. No one could drink it. Otto swore the color changed the temperature and the flavor.

When I was a kid, I tried putting blue food coloring in a glass of milk and stirring it up. I tried to drink it, but I couldn't. It just wasn't natural. Go ahead. Try it. Let me know if you fare better.

The creative mind is always experimenting. It puts pieces together to see what can be made. It takes things apart to see how they work. It adds components to see what will happen. It generates and manipulates and speculates and contemplates. Sometimes it achieves success, sometimes failure. But, as Edison said, failure is just another form of success, because now you know how *not* to do something.

⊞　⊞　⊞

When does it begin, this creative, experimenting mind? I picture an as-yet unborn child making cave drawings on the womb wall with its toes as it speculates what the outside world must look like, or doing experiments in the best thumb-sucking techniques. "Hmm, sideways or vertical? Fingers extended or fingers curled?"

Okay, maybe it doesn't start quite *that* young, but it does start young. And the younger a brain is, the less inhibited it is and the more likely it is to explore. Kids begin to rein in their creativity with the introduction of each new rule. I worry that our traditional educational system stresses the need to fit in and to follow along too much, and it beats the creativity out of our kids. As most adults know, it can sometimes be difficult to hang onto creativity, ingenuity, and inventiveness.

When Rupert was three, he tried roasting a pen in the toaster and lighting a match in his closet. At that point, we introduced a couple of strictly enforced rules into his life—e.g., no putting pens or other non-food objects into toasters (especially when the toaster is plugged in), and no matches for three-year-old boys unless Mom or Dad are directly supervising and aware that the three-year-old has matches in his possession.

This put an end to Rupert's experiments with toasters and matches. We realize that we may have inhibited his creativity a titch, but we felt that the long-term benefits outweighed any new information he would gain by continuing to pursue those specific activities.

Why was Rupert experimenting with the toaster and matches? Was he a budding arsonist? Did he crave ink-flavored toast? Was he a troublemaker? No. Just a curious boy.

When Rupert's cousin Fritzie was four, she and a cohort, another four-year-old girl, managed to vandalize some bedrooms by breaking some objects, gluing some pictures to the wall and carpet, and cutting each other's hair with child safety scissors. Why did they do this? Were they inherently naughty? No. They just didn't have the experience yet to understand the consequences. They were doing their thing, unaware of a parental reaction to follow. They were curious. The judgment part of their brains hadn't kicked in. It usually doesn't until about age 18, and sometimes later than that.

Life in the fast brain may mean that your motives are sometimes misunderstood, especially when you are a child who does not have the vocabulary or understanding, or even the voice, to defend yourself. We've often heard that being smart is not an excuse for bad behavior. But guess what—sometimes it is. Sometimes the fault lies not in the behavior but in the perception of the behavior.

Did Rupert really intend to burn down our house and all of our belongings? Of course not; he just wanted to see what would happen if he lit a match. He wanted to know if he was capable of operating that thing and what else he could use it for or make it do. He was curious. When I smelled the sulfur and hunted down the source, I quickly explained to Rupert exactly what a match was capable of doing and forbade him from touching them again without my permission—but I didn't punish him. I want him to be curious. I also want him to understand safety precautions. If he would have done it again, after he was fully aware of the danger of the situation, well *then* there would have been some serious consequences.

It was the same when he put the pen in the toaster. He was not a miniature version of an evil, mad scientist, but simply a naïve kid with a brain that wanted to know more and more and more and "what will happen if?"

When Fritzie and company were breaking things in the bedrooms, were they intentionally vandalizing? Or did one of them say to the other, "Hey, look, this thing can bend!"

"Wow, see how far it will bend! Keep going!"

Snap. Oops. Oh well, next experiment!

Or were they playing a game of their own invention, and it got a little out of control?

Yes, they need to learn to respect the property of others, but that's just the point—they need to *learn* it. They don't always have a natural grasp of that concept. Their little brains are outpacing their maturity and understanding, and what are they supposed to do with all of that curiosity and creativity that's running loose and begging to be used? They haven't yet developed enough self-control to tell it to sit tight until they receive further instructions.

When they were gluing pictures to the carpet and the wall, they innocently believed that they were making the world a better place—at least until they saw the look on an adult's face. That's when learning suddenly stepped in. "Oops. She isn't pleased. Perhaps this was not the best choice."

My nephew Harvey was about four when his mother noticed a stench coming from a storage room in the basement. After a little searching, she discovered an old puddle of smashed, raw (but by now dried up) eggs. Their kitchen, which was directly above, was being remodeled, and a drain hole remained exposed. Harvey noticed that this drain hole was just big enough for an egg to pass through, and how could he pass up such a cool opportunity to learn something about gravity and impact? He would drop an egg down and quickly put his eye to the hole to see what happened, but he wasn't quick enough, and it was pretty dark down there, so he tried it again. And again. And again.

It was not Harvey's intention to drive his mom crazy and create a bad smell in the basement. It was his intention to learn something. That's a good thing. And learn he did. He discovered that mothers do not appreciate their houses smelling like rotten eggs, and they really *despise* having to clean up dried egg mess. Harvey may have been curious if those two new and fascinating discoveries held true in every situation. For example, if he were to pour his uneaten cold cereal and milk down the hole, would it smell as bad as the eggs did? How long would it take his mom to discover the new mess? Questions, always questions.

Again, that's a good thing—as long as kids understand the complete reasoning behind the rules as well.

⊞   ⊞   ⊞

We don't want to give fast and busy brains so many rules that it slows down their questioning; we just want to make sure that they, as well as our personal belongings and our sanity, are protected from harm or injury.

This winter, we didn't use our wood stove very often, so I had to content myself with warming my hands over the soft, warm, smoky glow of the lamp on my end table. Thanks to Rupert, who discreetly placed his chewed-up gum on the top of the lightbulb, we can now enjoy the scent as well as the wispy visuals of smoke rising from what was once an ordinary electrical appliance.

I've talked to him about the potential danger and the harm of playing with a lamp or any other heat-producing or electrical appliances. However, I remember when I was a kid, I did the same thing with crayons. I wanted to know what would happen, darn it. I didn't want to ask, and I didn't want to be told, I wanted to find out, to discover on my own. I still remember how cool it was to watch the melted crayons thin and bubble down the side of the bulb and to watch them change color as they burned and darkened or melted together. At that stage of my life, I found it fascinating. I wasn't trying to create a fire hazard or produce a smelly, smoky ambiance for the rest of the family to enjoy. My brain was hungry for information, and it relished and consumed every information-gathering experiment I could invent.

I see that gum in the glass chimney of my beautiful table lamp, and I watch the tiny tendrils of smoke rise and cloud the glass. As an adult, I'm embarrassed that my table lamp has a wad of melting gum attached to the inside, and I think I need to do some problem solving and figure out how to get it out of there and clean the lamp chimney. Then, the kid in me remembers, and I think, "I've got a pretty cool son. I know just how he feels. I wonder what he learned from that experiment? Did he hang his head over the top of the lamp and watch in wonder as the gum transformed and sizzled?" I hope he doesn't burn the house down, but I hope he doesn't quit experimenting. That first-hand experience is one of the best ways to collect information.

⊞ ⊞ ⊞

Sometimes we look at the nice, quiet child as the "good" child, the "easy" child. We look at the children who know how to fit in, and we recognize how fortunate they are to have that skill, because not all of us do. They don't do anything odd. They follow all the rules. They appear to be well-behaved.

Never confuse conformity with "good behavior." As a mom, I appreciate good behavior, but I consider experimenting (within the bounds of safety), testing theories, and going out on a limb when necessary to be "good behavior" as well. Sitting in class, or anywhere else, and following all of the rules and complying with every social norm and trend and thought is "empty behavior." I don't want my children to be content with a strict diet of someone else's ideas. I don't want them to only digest what they are fed; I want them to feed themselves and to obtain their own sustenance.

Rupert, who has been fascinated with robots for quite some time, brought me one of his toys when he was six—a microscope that projects images onto an attached screen. He had taken it apart to see how it worked and to use the parts to make something even better—like robots. He'd been rather bored with that toy anyway.

The budget-conscious and proper left-brained parent side of me almost said, "Rupert, you can't take your toys apart. We paid good money for that!" Thankfully, the creative I-remember-what-it-was-like-to-be-a-kid-and-be-curious side of me realized that this was a good thing. By taking it apart, he was learning more than he ever would have if he'd left that toy intact. His curiosity and creativity spurred him on to explore the inner makings of the toy world. How could I complain?

So the next thing I knew, Rupert was sitting at the dining room table surgically removing, with child safety scissors, the vinyl skin from a large mechanical dinosaur. I gulped as I watched the once fine specimen of a dinosaur undergo the knife of a skilled plastic-removal surgeon. Rupert's tongue hung out of his mouth as he concentrated on his operation. He wanted to get to the mechanical part of the toy. All that lifelike skin was in his way. As he worked, he announced, "Man, I can't believe they make these things so easy to take apart!"

I have to admit, the dinosaur robot that he ultimately exposed was much cooler than the original toy, and Rupert now had a robot to study as it moved so he could watch how the parts worked together.

Later, I walked into his room to find a stringless badminton racket, a pair of scissors, and a worried-looking Rupert.

"I'm making something special out of it," he said.

"Like what?"

"It's hard to explain."

I took a quick glance around the room to look for other items that might have been demolished or "reinvented." I took a deep breath. These are his toys. His brain has other uses for them. Just as I had allowed the now-skinless dinosaur, I had to relinquish control of the rest of his belongings. Well, maybe just his toys. If he started taking apart the furniture, I would have to put my foot down.

It's one thing to teach my kids how to take care of things, but it's another thing to attempt to put a leash on an inventive brain. The toys are his. They were purchased for his enjoyment. The only rules are that he can't throw them in the house and he can't leave them all over the yard. If he prefers to disassemble them and build his own toys, well, as long as he cleans up after himself, I can't really say anything.

He has been given rules about the dangers of electrical appliances and about causing damages to someone else's property. He has boundaries. I need to let him work within those boundaries.

⊞　⊞　⊞

Pandora's room has experienced times when it's rigged up so that only she knows how to open the door safely. Her room appears to have just experienced a catastrophic event—maybe a hurricane or a tornado, which would explain the scarves and jump ropes strewn from shelf to shelf to her doorknob until it looks as if some giant spider has been building a nest. I'm afraid if I pull on one end of her handiwork, the whole room will unravel.

It's a creative, if inefficient, security system.

I want her to learn how to keep her room clean and tidy. This is a good skill to have. But I also want her to have opportunities to create and experiment. I have to discover ways to find a balance. I make rules that allow her to rig up her contraptions, but I limit her to a certain time period, like maybe a week, and then she has to clean them up, because I know that otherwise, one experiment will pile on another and another until we have heaps of absolute havoc.

Lately, she has taken to keeping her room clean and saving her contraptions for an outside fort. I can live with that. Her brain is free to experiment, so she's happy too.

Adults aren't that much different than children. Their brains still yearn for firsthand information; they want to experiment and find out "What happens if…." Our familiarity of "the rules" has both freed us and inhibited us. Most of us are well aware of the dangers of electricity, so we can take precautions to protect ourselves when we take apart a piece of machinery. However, our familiarity with "the rules" also tells us that we need to live in fear that we might break something or we won't be able to put something back together. "The rules" may also inhibit us from pursuing questions that our friends or family are uncomfortable with.

There are many ways to learn. There is a world of things to learn about. There are zillions of discoveries that have yet to be made, even if it's only on an individual basis. Experiment. Find out for yourself. Take surveys. Test theories. Your brain is growling. It's hungry. It wants to know. Feed it.

10: Feeling Different and Fitting In

When Magnolia was ready to begin kindergarten, she decided to go in style, so she lopped off her bangs with a pair of scissors two days before school began, and then the day before arriving in her classroom, she sucked on a plastic cup until her lips were a lovely shade of semi-permanent cornflower blue. I think it was her way of counting down the days until school started—her own physically interactive advent calendar. I was grateful she wasn't much good at counting past two.

She might as well have had "I'm gifted" tattooed on her forehead. Oh sure, lots of children experiment with scissors and hair, and sucking on a cup isn't all that unusual, either. But gifted children do have a tendency to stand out from the crowd in one way or another—whether it's because of their advanced intellectual skills or because they just seem unexplainably different from the rest of the bunch. Sometimes there are obvious clues, like Magnolia's physical expressions of her busy and curious mind. Other times it's more subtle, and it only makes itself known with time. Sometimes the only person who is aware of the differentness is the child herself.

I remember that feeling from my elementary school years— you look at everyone else and you smile and try to act normal, but you know you aren't. If you haven't been identified as "gifted," or "talented," then you don't know what to call yourself or why you're so different. You feel isolated, because you're afraid to spill out too many of your ideas, since your friends will look at you with that weird look that happens every time you open your mouth with an unconventional response. You want to fit in, but most attempts just seem to aggravate the situation. The safest route appears to be to smile a lot, don't call attention to yourself, and for Pete's sake, all those bizarre ideas in your head should probably stay there until you can find a kindred spirit who will understand.

I was quiet and shy during most of my younger years. I spoke out on occasion, but I usually regretted it. I had friends, but most of them didn't know the real me. The real me is weird. The real me…I remember her from the early-early years, before I discovered the desire to fit in.

The real me, when I played outside on snowy winter days, would lie face up on a picnic table for what seemed like hours and feel the cold seep through my clothing while I watched the clouds drift against the blue sky above me. I would dig a hole in the snow, and then I would stick my head in up to my neck like an ostrich so I could watch the snow melt inside the hole as my breath flew against it. Talk about brain freeze!

I wonder what the neighbors thought when they drove by our house and saw a headless child bending over the snow and holding as still as a statue.

Maybe this is normal behavior for a little kid. All I know is that when my friends came over, none of *them* wanted to bury their heads in the snow. And certainly, when I went to first grade, no one else on the playground was doing that sort of thing.

When friends came over to my house, I would say, "Let's just make up our own recipes and see what happens!" or, "Let's pretend that this hillside is…." My friends would look at me and shake their heads. Then they would suggest something more conventional.

I was always eager to go to their houses and learn more of what "conventional" was. My little brain would think, "Ohhhh, so *this* is what civilized people do!" They made cookies with all of the usual ingredients. Their food looked like normal food. Their bedrooms were usually clean and tidy, without a hodge-podge of projects taking up floor space, and they were organized and had store-bought comforters instead of homemade patchwork crazy quilts. They played with the actual Barbie toy accessories instead of inventing their own. Their mothers didn't wear paint-smattered clothing; instead, they wore clothing like what I saw in the J.C. Penney's catalogs. Not Stepford families by any means, but certainly conventional families who knew how to act, what to wear, what to think. I felt like a foreigner in their midst.

Part of me rebelled, as I desperately wanted to cling to my own original—if strange and somewhat eccentric—ways, and a part of me went underground until I felt it was safe to come out.

I rebelled in ways that expressed my desire to be an individual, but in ways that I perceived as safe socially. For example, I wore conventional and what I perceived to be stylish clothes, though my taste was no doubt skewed by my lack of ability to appreciate "normal." I insisted on wearing dresses every day when everyone else wore jeans. Normal, but different.

▦ ▦ ▦

I find myself encouraging my children to fit in while also encouraging them to be different. I try to buy them normal clothing. I try to teach them social skills like good manners to help them fit in with the rest of the world. I don't want them to have to feel like an outsider exploring strange territory. They have to be able to relate to others if they want to communicate and work with other people. That's just the way it is. If you can't relate, you can't communicate, and if you can't communicate, how lonely is that? How can you function?

However, I still encourage them to be different—not simply for the sake of being different and proving that they are unique, but to allow them to follow their passions and interests and to unchain their brains from the fetters of convention.

Stanley, my oldest, seems to defy convention at every turn. Not only does he have his own sense of fashion, but he has his own sense of self. He *loves* being different. He's not very tall, he doesn't tan, and he doesn't have rippling biceps. His favorite shirt says, "Chicks dig pale, scrawny guys." He does what he calls "snow-angel break dancing." Stanley can't help himself. He isn't conventional. He will never be conventional. He has no desire to be conventional.

Fortunately, Stanley has a strong group of friends—peers who feel the same way he does. He has people who can, at least in part, relate to him. When he and his friends were in high school, they started "Suit Tuesdays" and "Casual Suit Fridays" so they could wear all of the funky polyester suits that they found at the local free clothing store. They began their own club. One artistic friend made T-shirts with caricatures of Stanley's head on various animal bodies, and they all wore these to school. Most of Stanley's friends in high school were bright, talented boys. They were different. They stood out. They were proud to stand out. And they laughed at each other's jokes. Stanley was lucky to have those friends.

⊞　⊞　⊞

Rupert, my youngest, has yet to find peers who understand him. He seems to get along well with most children, but he's only in first grade. He has yet to form connections with like-minded peers. However, I am beginning to wonder if he *has* any like-minded peers. Oh sure, he can pull in the other boys with his plans to save the reald, but how many other boys his age get excited about scrubbing things?

I took Rupert to the grocery store with me when he was about five. As I stood there examining the mops, Rupert perused the items at his eye level—and found a treasure.

"Can I get this, Mom, pleeeease? I'll pay you back when we get home!" He had all of seven dollars and seven cents to his name. I know this, because he counted it so often. He likes counting money. He likes anything to do with math or money.

Rupert stood there in the store holding a plastic all-purpose scrubber with a tube attached to it to hold soapy water that fed directly into the sponge. It was a cheap little gadget, but Rupert was in love. I asked, "Are you sure you want that? Do you know what it's used for?"

"Yeah, scrubbing."

"And if I get that for you, do you promise to use it to help scrub bathrooms and floors and all manner of other items?"

He looked at me earnestly. "Yes, Mom, I promise."

How could I resist? "Okay," I said. "I'll get it for you. My treat."

"Yessss!"

So Rupert temporarily forgot his plans for protecting his ninja castle with cannons, sticks, and bows and arrows (he said guns were too dangerous), and entered a new housecleaning phase. He scrubbed the counters and then hopped into the tub and gave it a good scrub-down. He showed everyone the minute they walked into the door. "Look what I got today!" I felt like saying the same thing.

The next morning, he came and jumped into bed with Hubby and me—scrubber in hand. He waved it around in a circular motion. In a high-pitched "let's pretend" voice, he said, "Scrub, scrub, scrub."

He was a self-professed cleaning superhero. "Brush your teeth, brush your teeth, brush your teeth," he said to Magnolia. He was going to drive her crazy. A few minutes earlier, he told her to clean her room as he scrubbed the front of the dishwasher. Now that's the kind of guy I want fighting on my team—a "grime-fighter"!

How many of his five-year-old friends were likely to jump at an invitation to play "spring cleaning" at Rupert's house?

A couple of weeks ago, as we were contemplating putting our house on the market to sell, I had asked Rupert, "How would you feel if we moved?"

He sighed. "Oh, I think that would be great. You know, it's just so much easier to keep a house clean if it starts off that way."

This was not the response I had anticipated. "What about your friends?"

"I can always make new ones."

Now, lest you get the wrong idea about Rupert, I have to say that he loves a clean house, and he likes to scrub on occasion, but please, do not expect a clean room should you ever visit our home. His room is his workshop and personal museum. No matter how many times we muck it out, it immediately returns to its original, seemingly chaotic state. I wanted to remind him of this when he made the comment about a house being easier to clean if it starts out that way, because his room starts out that way on a regular basis, and it doesn't seem to do him any good. However, I refrained from saying anything. Maybe if he believes that statement enough, eventually it will come to pass.

As I mentioned earlier, hope is what keeps me going.

⊞　⊞　⊞

Another thing that keeps me going is the enjoyment of the differentness, the not fitting in, the unconventional. I've learned to value it rather than be embarrassed by it—at least most of the time.

My nephew Roland is an 11-year-old boy who started life with some handicaps. He suffered a stroke before he was even born, and as a result, his brain did not develop properly. He has something called Dandy Walkers Syndrome, and his physical coordination is very poor. He walks in his own odd, jerking manner. He's a sweet kid. He'll sit and watch Care Bears with his four-year-old sister. He is also a bright kid; he tests four years above his age across the board in every subject.

To top it all off—and this is the best part—he's a *happy* kid. Roland understands what he is dealing with, and he doesn't seem to mind being different. He doesn't match his age peers emotionally, intellectually, or physically, and yet he is well-adjusted and happy with himself. At recess one day, the playground teacher noticed him leaping around on the pavement and asked, "Roland, what are you doing?"

"I'm dodging sunbeams!" Roland answered with his usual cheerfulness.

It appears that in Roland's world, no matter how many strikes he has against him or how different he is, the sunbeams are plentiful. You can see them in his smile. My sister deserves credit for helping him be content with himself.

🏶 🏶 🏶

I relish living in a world of the unexpected, where there is rarely a dull moment. The other day, I knocked on my sister Edna's door, and her third-grade daughter Wilhelmina opened it just wide enough to poke her head out. "Friend or foe?"

It's the little things like that that make me smile. It's not the usual greeting.

🏶 🏶 🏶

Pandora is an odd one and proud of it. She used to be more reserved, but lately she has taken to becoming a drama queen of the humorous kind. She is always ready to entertain with one of her impressions, whether she's performing for a familiar audience of friends and family or for total strangers. When she did her Barney the Dinosaur impression for a woman we didn't know, I whispered to my husband, "You know how some kids, when they get older, want their parents to drop them off two blocks away from the high school, because they're embarrassed to be seen with their parents?"

"Yeah."

"Well, I have a feeling that you and I will be dropping off Pandora two blocks away from the high school so we can protect our *own* identities."

And yet I really am proud of her—even if sometimes I prefer to be proud of her from a distance. I love that she feels so confident, so uninhibited. In that way, she is my hero. I watched her with two older girls who didn't know her. Pandora is in fourth grade; these two girls were in sixth. Pandora sat down next to them and began her goofiness. Their first reaction was to look at each other and roll their eyes. Pandora seemed unaware of their disdain, and she kept right on going. A couple hours later, I saw these same two girls eating lunch with Pandora and laughing with her, not just at her. They'd warmed up to her. She had persisted in being herself, and after the initial shock wore off, the girls seemed to actually enjoy her ability to just be herself.

Sometimes it is a shock to just see people be themselves and act naturally—especially when giftedness comes into play and brains that are wired differently expose their true identities. As a society, we've become so used to keeping up appearances and fitting in that we're not used to seeing anything else. But what a fresh experience it is to meet someone who feels comfortable in her own skin!

We need to get used to our own skins, our own thoughts, our own ideas, talents, and gifts. We need to explore them, to make the most of them, to not be ashamed of them. We shouldn't trade them in for the average or the norm. As adults, we need to watch the example we set for our children and review the expectations with which society limits us. Are those expectations valid and worthy? Sift through them. Chuck any unnecessary ones.

⊞　⊞　⊞

When Magnolia was five, all she wanted for Christmas was a ream of clean white paper. That was it. As parents, we knew society expected us to provide something more than a ream of copy paper, so we bought her a desk to go with it. We didn't know if she'd like a desk, but for Pete's sake, we had to do something. We didn't want to look neglectful or cheap. Magnolia was thrilled to find the desk the next morning, but only because a ream of copy paper was sitting on it. The desk was like the wrapping paper and the boxes—the extra stuff that gets discarded when we clean things up.

When my niece Minerva was four, all she wanted was the wrapping paper. So that's what her wise mom gave her—a roll or two of wrapping paper. Her mother didn't slyly give her the wrapping paper wrapped around a toy, but she gave it to her straight out. That's what the girl wanted; that's what the girl got. There was no need to impress friends.

⊞   ⊞   ⊞

My brother Myron has always had a pretty strong sense of self. He is who he is, and he doesn't try to be anything different for anyone. You get what you see. He says what he thinks. His wife first discovered this when she went on a date with him and they were walking by a restaurant with outdoor seating. As they passed by a family of diners, Myron said, "Hey, those nachos look delicious."

The father said, "You're welcome to have some."

So Myron said, "Don't mind if I do," and he grabbed a couple and went on his way, with his future wife slightly embarrassed and yet impressed. He wanted to taste the nachos. They were offered, and he accepted. He didn't think twice about putting on a pretense and saying, "Oh, no, that's okay. They look good, but I'm not really hungry. Thanks anyway."

If only we all had the courage to say what we think and be who we are. How many great thoughts are being swept under the rug because they might embarrass us if our neighbors see them?

⊞   ⊞   ⊞

I know of one young man who is the son of a doctor. I'll call him Larry. Apparently, Larry has some interest in his dad's profession, because he knows a thing or two about the medical world—and he's not afraid to let other people know what's on his mind. In grade school, he was on the bus one day when some other kids began making fun of a little girl with Down's

Syndrome. Larry said to those kids, "Hey, do you even know what Down's Syndrome is? She can't help what she's got!" And he proceeded to explain in detail exactly what Down's Syndrome was. Those other kids received a bit of an education. They had a better understanding of Down's Syndrome, and they also learned a little bit about standing up for other people— and that knowledge can be a powerful thing.

As a teenager, Larry has been known to wear a wristband that says "Endometriosis" on it. He's not afraid to voice his opinion or his thoughts. He's who he is. Take it or leave it.

🏳 🏳 🏳

When people read *Raisin' Brains* and write to me on my website, I get one of two responses. Readers either ask in disbelief, "Did all of that stuff *really* happen in your family?" or they say, "That book reminded me of *my* family. My family is really weird, too!"

There are a lot of us out there, mixing and mingling with perfectly normal people. Some of us have learned to blend in so well that others would never suspect the oddness and the divergent thinking that happens in our heads or in our homes. How many kindred spirits are out there, hiding behind faces of convention and normalcy?

A kindergartener wrote a love poem to the girl of his dreams. It read:

> *Dear Elizabeth Bernweilter,*
> *I love you with all my heart. In your head I see a brain.*
> *Love, Ferdinand*

This kid knew what he was looking for. He could sense Elizabeth's thinking patterns, and apparently, that outweighed all sense of physical beauty in his little mind.

We need to find each other so we can find peers to whom we can relate. In order to find each other, we need to be ourselves and not be afraid to be odd or different.

Coping with giftedness means accepting it for what it is and for who we are. It's a cool thing. It doesn't make us better than anyone else, because it's just a matter of a brain that works differently, but it does give us a unique experience in this life, and why keep that to ourselves?

We need to make sure that our children retain a sense of pride in who they are as an individual, that they *are* individuals, and that being different is really, really cool. There are some who are concerned with the label "gifted," but it can mean so many different things, and most of them are good things. "Gifted" or "talented" is not a label to be either ashamed of or flaunted, but to be understood and enjoyed.

When my nephew Parker was identified in third grade as a "gifted" or "advanced learning" child, the first thing he did was come home and make a sign to paste on his door—"Einstein at Work!" How cool is that? He had grasped a glimpse of his own potential, and it felt exhilarating and liberating for him.

When we learn to accept ourselves, our eccentricities, our differences and divergence, we will be well on our way to enjoying this trip of life in the fast brain!

11: Laughing It Off

My sister Darleen has a special needs child who is now 11 years old but is developmentally disabled. Opal is a sweet girl, curious, and adventurous. She has red hair and a crooked, sidewise smile, and she loves to laugh. Thankfully, she has been blessed with a family who loves to laugh also, because her antics could be a significant stress factor in less relaxed family situation.

Opal is a child who cannot quite wrap her brain around a lot of things, but she does know how to wreak what some people might refer to as havoc. A couple of years ago, she pulled the fire alarm at school and sent the entire elementary school into single-file lines out on the lawn. She was very proud of herself. Another morning, just before school, she covered her room, her clothing, her sheets, her blankets, and herself in black acrylic paint.

All Opal needs is a few minutes of unsupervised play time. I believe she plans ahead, just waiting for her mother or a sibling to get distracted so she can go to work and try new things.

One weekend, she managed to find a magic marker. No, she did not color the couch or the walls. She colored Binks, the wiener dog. He probably figured she was just giving him a nice little back scratch. But now he has a saddle-blanket tattoo. To make matters even more interesting, she gave him a lovely pair of eyebrows to go with it. Groucho Binks. All he needs is a cigar-shaped dog biscuit.

Permanent marker. Blue.

How does my sister cope with this? She calls us and she laughs. She tries not to laugh in front of Opal, because she doesn't want to encourage her, but after the commotion has died down, the embarrassment has worn off a little, and she has removed all of the black acrylic paint that is removable, she laughs. It not only saves her sanity, but it makes her love Opal even more, because she appreciates, rather than resents, the nutty experiences that Opal brings into her life. What would be the point of getting angry? Opal does the best she can.

Our attitudes make all the difference in the world.

※　※　※

I was presenting a keynote at a conference for gifted education teachers a few years back, and I was a little nervous. On my way into the ballroom where I was about to speak, I tripped over one of the vendors' book racks. I quickly recovered my dignity, grabbed a cup of water, and brought the water to a cloth-covered table in the front. I sat the cup down and flipped through my transparencies and papers to make sure I hadn't forgotten anything, because heavens to Betsy, I didn't want to look like a fool. I took a deep breath. The room was packed. I was their entertainment. Yikes!

Then I sat down at my table and watched an interesting phenomenon. My cup of water appeared to be racing unaided across the table and in the direction of my lap. Apparently, when I sat down in my chair, I managed to catch the end of the tablecloth, and the closer I got to the seat of my chair, the more tablecloth I pulled with me.

I caught the glass just in time, with only a few drops free to splatter across my suit. Whew! During the opening remarks, I sat waiting for the other shoe to drop. What would happen next? Would I trip over my own feet on my way up to the stage? My mind went back to my high school days when I walked across the floor of an auditorium full of my peers sitting in the bleachers waiting for an assembly, and I tripped over a microphone cord in front of the entire crowd. Then my mind went back even further to second grade, when I stepped off the bus at school and the kid behind me stepped on the hem of my elastic-waisted skirt. I ended up flat on my face on the school lawn, skirtless and skivvied.

The horror of that moment replayed in my mind as I envisioned the same thing happening in front of this new crowd of peers. My insecure self began to take over.

Thank goodness my sensible self stepped in to save the day. It said, "Karen, you're here to talk about humor, right?"

"Right."

"So this could turn out to be one of the moments when you most need it, yes?"

"Yes."

"And how perfect is that? You'll have a chance to exercise one of your favorite coping skills in front of your audience. You can practice what you preach."

And I thought, "You know, that's true!"

The good news is that this time, I didn't trip on my way up to the stage—and the other good news is that I realized that I was right in the middle of a potential laughter moment, which helped lower my stress level a little. Any mistake or clumsiness on my part was just one more opportunity to talk about the benefits of handling life with humor.

⊞ ⊞ ⊞

Last summer I was heading down the highway when a deer ran in front of my minivan and smashed my windshield. My first reaction was confusion. I pulled over to the side of the road for a minute to gather my senses. Glass was everywhere. When I closed my mouth, I could feel the glass grinding between my teeth. I realized later that I was apparently in some sort of shock. I turned around and drove home in a complete daze, which was dangerous. I was shaking. I had to lean all of the way to the right to see out my front window, which was also dangerous. When I got home, I shook the glass out of my clothes and had a bit of a cry as the shock wore off and I contemplated my recent experience.

That afternoon, when I drove my kids home from school (in another car), Otto pointed out as we pulled into the driveway that the rearview mirror on my minivan was missing and there were large dents all of the way down the side of it. Terrific. I had been too shaken to notice those things earlier. Then, as we were getting out of the car, I slammed the car door on my hand, proving that I was still not all together and able to function properly.

Later that evening, when I spoke with my friend Patrice on the phone, she asked me how my day had been. I mentioned that I hit a deer and totaled my van. She laughed. She laughed louder with every detail. When I mentioned shutting my hand in the door, she really hollered.

I thought, "You know, I *like* Patrice. We have the same warped sense of humor. What a relief to have someone I can laugh about this with!"

In those few moments on the phone, the situation changed from a traumatic event to an experience to be shared with good friends. It became a bit of excitement—though not something I would ever intentionally choose to experience again. It became a story opportunity.

※ ※ ※

Of course, there are appropriate times to laugh, and times when it is best not to laugh. A little sensitivity is required; a little judgment is necessary.

I come from a family where all kinds of laughs are valued— belly laughs, chuckle laughs, smile at the corner of the mouth laughs. That is how we cope with the many things that make us or our children feel different. On many occasions, it is how we cope with stress. It's a lot more pleasant to laugh than it is to cry, and somehow, laughter is therapeutic. It clears your mind and revives your soul, especially when you can share the laughter with someone else.

In the days immediately after the September 11 attacks, I spent a lot of time in tears. I hate that part of me, because I feel as if I have no control over it. I don't want to cry, but still, the tears come, and I feel powerless to stop them. My family and I were at a church service when the terrorist attacks were mentioned. I started bawling uncontrollably—quietly, thankfully—but uncontrollably. I leaned over to Stanley, who was seated next to me, and asked him if he had a tissue. He pulled a crumpled wad of tissue out of his pocket and handed it to me.

Now I must tell you, I am a very squeamish and wimpy person with an overactive imagination. I do not share food or dishes with anyone, not even my children, and I most certainly do not share tissues. It's all I can do to keep my brain from imagining what those tissues have been through. So I looked at that tissue and asked Stanley, "Has this been used?"

He leaned over and whispered, "Only on one side."

And then a magical thing happened. I laughed! And it felt so good! The tears stopped flowing. I still felt sorrow over what had happened, but I had regained my composure and my perspective. I was once again in a position to appreciate life's little ironies, to smile at silliness. The world had not ended after all. Thank you, Stanley. I needed that just then.

🏶 🏶 🏶

On another occasion, when Otto was about 13, my husband and I were out enjoying a little time alone together when Otto called on me on my cell phone.

"Uh, Mom?"

I didn't like the sound of his voice. I knew something was wrong. "What, Otto?"

"Well, I was just walking down the stairs normally, and my toe went through the wall."

"What?! How?"

"I don't really know how it happened. My foot must have hit a weak spot in the sheetrock or something, because my toe just went right through it."

So Hubby and I drove home envisioning a two- or three-inch hole at the base of the wall on the stairway. It was some-what understandable. Somewhat. Otto was a big kid with big feet, and his usual way of walking down the stairs did sort of resemble his soccer slide tackles.

When we got home, imagine our surprise to see a giant, foot-shaped hole about five feet off the ground above the stair landing. It was covered with clear packing tape, as Otto and his friend thought that maybe if they patched it up a bit, it wouldn't look so bad.

We began with a barrage of parent questions and commentary, such as, "You were just walking down the stairs like you normally do and yet the hole is five feet off the ground?" or, "I thought that only your toe went through!" or, "A weak spot in the sheetrock?"

To which Otto replied, "Well, yeah," as if it all made perfect sense to him.

We gave him a brief lecture on appropriate inside-the-house behavior and the cost of repairing sheetrock, and then we retreated into the privacy of our bedroom—and we laughed. No, we weren't thrilled about the situation, but Otto's earnest explanation was so ridiculous that we couldn't help ourselves. We tried to be stern with him, but we did not go to bed angry that night.

Humor has helped get us through broken glass, broken light fixtures, more holes in the walls, and more sheetrock repair bills, all thanks to Otto. He's a physically active kid, and our house was designed for regular, civilized human behavior. His apologies were always so sincere and his stories were always so bizarre that we often had to stifle smiles—though paying the repair bills did help to sober us up a bit.

⊞ ⊞ ⊞

Laughter is a terrific way to not take ourselves or others too seriously. As a mom, I want my children to take me seriously, but I do not want to be in a constant state of uptightness. We have rules and we have fun, but we need both.

When Otto was in high school, he had a good friend named Farley who always wore his pants down around his hiney-hoo so that everyone could see which boxers he was wearing that day. I liked Farley, but this so-called fashion statement drove me crazy. Farley was also a neighbor, so we saw him fairly often, and it was not unusual for us to be giving him a ride to a soccer game or home from school. Farley knew I didn't appreciate the boxer briefing that we received every time we were in his presence. He knew this because before he hopped in our van, I would say something like, "Farley, you can't get in until you pull those pants up." I'd honk at him as he was walking home from the bus stop and motion for him to pull his pants up. I tried to be good-natured about it, because I wasn't out to rule his life. I just wanted to make a point—I didn't care what color and print his boxers were; it was too much information.

One afternoon, the phone rang. I answered it and heard Farley's voice. "Is Mr. or Mrs. Isaacson there?"

I said, "I don't know. Do you have your pants pulled up?"

There was silence on the other end of the phone.

An awful realization scooted across my brain. I said, "This isn't Farley, is it."

The voice on the other end of the line said, "No."

I stammered and apologized.

The cool thing was that I was later able to share this story with Farley, who happened to think it was hilarious and that I'd gotten what I deserved. It also helped keep our relationship light and kept my nagging from becoming, well, too much nagging. After that, whenever I asked Farley to pull up his pants (I made sure never to mention it over the phone again), Farley accommodated with a laugh. When I drove by him on the street, he didn't wait for me to make my usual motions, he just hitched his pants up, as if to say, "I know you're there" and kept walking.

⊞　⊞　⊞

Laughter is an admission that we're human; it gives us all permission to continue as mere imperfect mortals. Laughter is an acceptance that life is unpredictable, thank goodness, and enjoyable. Fast, gifted brains often have keen senses of humor, and that is truly a gift! To bring a smile to someone's face, to distract from the ordinary or the painful, to make everyday life more alive—this is not a gift to be taken lightly! Or perhaps that is exactly what it is.

Life with Stanley is always life with wit. He appreciates every little opportunity to make life fun and good. When he showed up at work wearing two different shoes, he was okay with that. He could see that it was kind of funny, and others were free to laugh.

Humor is the lens through which Stanley views life. When he worked at McDonald's and was in the process of changing the ketchup in the ketchup dispenser, he suddenly found himself standing in the middle of the floor wrestling with a large bag of ketchup spewing streams of red sauce in every direction. He felt a little foolish, but he said it was worth the smile on his manager's face. It was also a relief to know that he would never be asked to change out the ketchup dispenser again.

When he was in high school, Stanley was involved in Speech and Debate—always pursuing the humorous competitions, of course. But at the beginning of the year, his coach asked everyone to fill out an interest survey. When I went to parent-teacher conference, his Speech coach said, "You've got to see Stanley's interest survey."

She pulled a crinkled yellow paper (all of Stanley's school papers are crinkled—it's his personal trademark and a sign that the paper has passed through his locker or his backpack). I looked over the paper, which was filled out in Stanley's familiar nearly-impossible-to-read chicken scratch. He had answered all of the questions, but when he got to the end, the final portion of the survey asked, "Is there anything else we should know about you? Please comment."

Stanley wrote:

> *I'm a nice, sensitive, handsome SWM, 18. I enjoy long walks on the beach, horseback riding, reading by the fireplace, cuddling, movies, music. Non-smoker, non-drinker. Searching for SWF, 16-97, similar interests. Friendship first, possibly more. 097F Alpha 762090972.*

Stanley has been known to entertain our family with his monologues when we have taken long car trips. If he warms up to company at the dinner table, which doesn't always happen, we don't have to worry about conversation—we have to worry about our guests losing their drinks through their noses.

When Stanley reads stories to Rupert, a crowd gathers round, as his character voices grab our attention and make us forget about whatever it was we had been doing before we walked into the room and heard him reading. Rupert, of course, loves the dramatic reading. Story time with Stanley is never boring.

When we play games together as a family, it is always more fun when Stanley is there. He gets us started on a sing-along, and before we know it, we're singing "Someone Left My Cake Out in the Rain" or "Kung Foo Fighting" at the top of our lungs. He plays to win, but ultimately, it's about the playing. If he loses, he loses with flair. When he was younger, he couldn't play hide-and-seek because he couldn't stop giggling and he couldn't stand the suspense. He would jump up giggling and shout, "Here I am!"

Stanley is a different kind of kid, but that difference lights up lots of faces. And just when we think we're used to him, he surprises us again. His brain is in a constant state of discovery and always hungry for more—more irony, more wit, and more divergent discoveries to take him off the beaten path. He is an explorer of the world, and he is in search of precious specimens of humor.

☷ ☷ ☷

Fast brains can't resist humor—not even the really "cool" fast brains. When my husband and I recently took a trip out of state, we offered to bring my 11-year-old nephew Jordan back with us, and to take a recent high school graduate, Ernie, to the airport where he was leaving for college. Ernie was cool. He had a fast brain. He was nice enough, but I didn't think he was looking forward to a long drive with two boring adults and an 11-year-old boy who was consumed with a passion for Digi-mon cards. Ernie exercised a great deal of patience and listened to many a tale about all of the Digi-mon characters, but I could tell he was bored out of his mind. To distract my nephew from his cards for just a few minutes, my husband and I began playing a pun game using homophones.

We threw some examples out to inspire my nephew. "What do you call a clearance on boats?"

"A sail sale!"

"What do you call a proud artery?"

"A vain vein!"

Ernie sat quietly in the back of the van while we called out homophones. I could feel the tension build back there until he couldn't take it anymore. He shouted out, "What do you call a really cool bug?"

"What?"

"A fly fly!"

We went on like that for miles. It saved all of us from Digi-mon.

☷ ☷ ☷

There are plenty of times when brains don't connect on the humor level. Fast-brain children often have more advanced

148

senses of humor, and their age peers are not always in a position to appreciate it—which reminds me of a sixth-grade teacher I know. She has a bit of a warped sense of humor. When she tried to share her humor with her students, however, they just sat in their desks and looked at her, unsure of how to react. Finally, she bridged the humor communication gap by saying, "Okay, when I'm telling a joke, I'll wiggle my fingers over my head so that you'll know I'm not serious."

So at least the kids would know when to laugh, even if they weren't sure what it was they were laughing about.

Speaking of a warped sense of humor, think of it this way: It's sort of like abstract art—you have to "get it" to appreciate it. Most people will walk by, take a look at the thing, and miss the point entirely. They'll shrug their shoulders and write it off as a fraud—something anyone could do in their garage on a Saturday afternoon. But really, if you know what to look for, you can understand the artist's view and translation.

Wit is a workout for the brain. It's a challenge. It's a reward. It's a gift. It's one of the best coping tools we have.

12: Pulling Together

L ife is tough when you live in a house full of fast-brained personalities.

If you take one gifted adult living alone, you're probably talking about a pretty interesting household. That individual will no doubt have a few quirks, like organizing his clothing according to color, style, and the day it was last worn, and every hanger will be spaced one inch apart. That individual may be intense. He may have an intense interest in rocks and have cupboards and shelves full of them. He may be highly sensitive. He may not be able to tolerate the smell of a not-so-clean bathroom but be equally unable to handle the smell of disinfectant. He may be a perfectionist who has a conniption fit if the furniture gets bumped out of place or if the carpet is vacuumed against the grain.

Now take that same household and add another member—another person, an adult—for instance, a woman with her own quirks. She may be highly creative and leave messes in her wake. Her mind may be so focused on projects that she is habitually late and her meals are irregular. She may be sensitive to the beauty of a sunset or the reflections of a prism but blissfully unaware of the havoc in her closet. She may love music but can't think of anything else when it is playing, so she likes to keep the house quiet. Too much of any kind of noise overloads her circuits.

Now add one more. Perhaps a son with a sense of humor and a passion for music, whether he's playing his drums or listening to the radio at top volume. He may be absent-minded and leave his towel on the back of the couch or forget where he put his homework—if he did it at all. He has a long list of foods he can't or won't eat because certain textures bother him.

Add a fourth—a daughter who loves animals, even if they smell funny and leave messes around the house, whether it's birdseed, wood shavings from a hamster cage, or something else. She is fiercely independent and doesn't like following rules that don't make sense to her. She talks incessantly. She is idealistic and expects perfection from everyone else.

Consider that all of these people are gifted, and they take their quirks to the extreme. If you add it all up, what do you get? Chaos. Confusion. The probability of a natural disaster. But, in fact, a family.

Now, mix up the idiosyncrasies a bit and add three more intense little personalities, and you get some idea of what life is like at our house—seven different varieties of fast brain. Sometimes we clash; sometimes we complement. But always, always, we gain strength in pulling together.

※ ※ ※

There is something magnificent about such an explosive combination that rises above the explosiveness and creates something greater than the sum of its parts. We learn from each other. We learn to love each other. We learn to appreciate those who are different from us. We learn to get over ourselves and see past our own needs, desires, and interests.

Ideally, your family, whether the members live in the same home or whether they are extended, whether they are related to you or consist of close friends, should be the one group of people who know and understand all of your idiosyncrasies, your weak spots, your most embarrassing moments, and with whom you know you are safe. They love you no matter what. They appreciate you as a whole instead of only liking the one or two parts of you that they know or that you are willing to expose.

There will be rough moments. There will be times of heartache. Sometimes your family can hurt you worse than anyone else can. But ultimately, if you pull together, your family is where your greatest strength will lie.

⊞ ⊞ ⊞

It's tough being a mom. It's embarrassing, stressful, and sometimes downright humiliating. It seems sometimes as though my children stay up at night thinking of ways to make my life more difficult.

Just yesterday, Pandora, Rupert, and I were headed down the road when Rupert said, "Mom, I'm supposed to grow up and get married, huh?"

I said, "Yes, Rupert. You're supposed to be a good dad and a good husband some day."

"Uh-huh. And I'm supposed to have difficults."

"Difficults?"

"Yeah, children are difficults, and life is full of difficults, right? We're supposed to have them."

At this point, Pandora burst out laughing, and Rupert became offended. I had to lecture Pandora on laughing while simultaneously lecturing Rupert on being too easily offended and reminding him that it was okay if people laughed at him sometimes. Then I said, "Rupert, children are not 'difficults.'" Okay, I was lying through my teeth. They *are* difficult, but that's not all they are. As I explained to Rupert, they are also amazing bundles of potential whose petals continuously unfold before our eyes, they give great hugs, and they basically make my life worth living, and I would do it all over again with each one of them if I could.

Still, there is no getting around the difficult part. And stressful. And embarrassing.

⊞ ⊞ ⊞

I remember one day last year when I asked Pandora if she was ready to go to school. Then I asked her if she was wearing clean clothes. This is a completely reasonable question to ask a nine-year-old who may or may not consider clean clothes a priority. After all, if you're going to play soccer at recess, you're just going to get them dirty all over again anyway.

She said "yes." And I trusted her.

I brought her to school. As we walked into the school building, I noticed that it was fairly obvious that her pants were not clean. It was too late to take her back to change, so I had to smile and fight the urge to send her with a note to her teacher that said, "Really, I'm not a bad mom. It's just that I wasn't wearing my glasses when we were at home this morning. I'm nearsighted. I couldn't see the details. Pandora really does have access to clean clothes. I promise. Please do not call social services!"

The day before that, we had a narrow miss. I gave her a once-over, and she looked just fine. Then she let down her guard and uncrossed her arms, only to expose a large rip in the front of her shirt.

Hey, it was one of her favorite shirts. She wasn't happy with me when I asked her to change it.

Recently, I overheard a parent who works in the schools comment on those poor, neglected children whose parents don't care about them and send them in dirty, ratty clothing. These words replay themselves in my mind as I send my children off into the world to be judged by other concerned adults. Those who judge my children are judging me. I find this stressful. I would appreciate it if my children fell in line and only did things that reflected well on me. Is that too much to ask?

Well, yes, it is. I have to remember that their purpose in life isn't to make me look good but to learn and grow, and in order to do that, they are going to have to make mistakes and do stupid things. And they're going to have their own personalities and their own desires, and what's that all about? I didn't sign up for that. (Did I sign up for that? I don't recall....)

Then again, I guess I did. I wasn't looking for carbon copies. I don't want to see my kids make all my same mistakes, and I so enjoy seeing them excel in ways I didn't.

🆘 🆘 🆘

Pandora may have a tendency to sneak out in her best soccer-playing clothes rather than clean, crisp, school clothes, but she also has a tendency to be a super thoughtful creature, always sensitive to the needs of others.

Last November, on the day after Thanksgiving, I rose at an ungodly hour and joined my three sisters for a long day of bargain shopping. We headed out into the dark morning, which could technically still be called "night," and mapped out the stores with the best deals on the things we were looking for. My body was running on adrenalin, because sleep had hardly entered the picture. Adrenalin and the feast from the day before.

Okay, yes, I am one of those people I like to mock—the after-Thanksgiving bargain-aholic. I used to swear I'd never stand in line for an hour in sub-freezing temperatures just so I could get a discount coupon for an item that I didn't need—I mean, that isn't what Christmas is all about, right?

Right. Nonetheless, by doing just that—standing in line in early morning hours—I saved $25 on an already crazily discounted doorbuster of a sale on an MP3 player for a child's Christmas gift. How about them apples?

Okay, so you can see now where I'm coming from. No sleep, too much food, and a frenzied mind. Pandora put two and two together. She thought about me and my needs. When I came home from our shopping trip, I found her washing dishes. She said she'd already cleaned the kitchen twice, cleaned the basement, made my bed, cleaned her room, sorted through some clutter on the dining room table, and cleaned out a drawer in the dining room. (I'm sure I've left out something.) She said she knew I'd be tired when I came home, and she didn't want me to have to come home to a messy house.

We had a house full of guests at the time, mostly small children, and it was no easy task to keep the place clean. But Pandora did it. She wanted to do it. She knew I'd be grateful. I *was*.

I was never that thoughtful as a child. How exciting to watch my just-turned-10-year-old daughter become such a fantastic and compassionate person! (And how exciting it was to crash in bed that day and know that the house was in good hands!)

⊞   ⊞   ⊞

On another occasion, when Rupert and Pandora were the only children at home with my husband and me, Pandora decided that we needed to have some fun together, so she planned a party for the four of us.

Pandora's party was interesting. She organized several homemade versions of carnival games, as well as a See Who Can Draw the Best Picture of Pandora Contest. The winners received prizes, which were objects she'd gathered from her room and no longer wanted. We then watched a homemade "movie" and an improvised play of "The Frog Prince" performed by Pandora and Rupert.

After a cheesecake intermission, Rupert entertained us with his version of Pandora's games and a five-second production of his own, which also involved a frog. He must have felt that since the first production had been such a success, the continuation of an amphibious theme would be a sure winner with his audience.

Hubby and I made out like bandits—not only did we score a piece of cheesecake, but I won a paintbrush, and Hubby won a large plastic lime-green dinosaur bank (emptied of its pennies) and a wind-up kids' meal toy.

I ask you, does life get any better than that?

⊞   ⊞   ⊞

I remember back when Pandora was three years old, she sat studiously drawing at the table. Some kids struggle with basic drawing skills at that age. If they can draw people, they usually skip a few parts, like the neck or even the body. I looked over

Pandora's tiny shoulder and gasped. She was drawing a picture of an intricate, multi-paneled table lamp. Not only was it easily recognizable, but it was in proportion and in perspective.

No, I do not love my children because of their accomplishments, but I have to admit, it is really exciting to discover their unique talents and capabilities. Every new accomplishment brings joy to their lives, even if the accomplishment is discovering that they can handle failure in a mature fashion and refuse to let it keep them down. If it brings joy to their lives, then it usually brings joy to mine.

⊞   ⊞   ⊞

When two-year-old Stanley began reading, without my help or knowledge, it was exciting. It's like you get a glimpse of all of the possibilities that you didn't even know existed. You look at the short person you helped to make, and you think, "Holy cow! What have I done? What is he going to do next? This is amazing!"

And every time I watch the world of reading unfold before my other children, even though none of the others started to read any earlier than the average child, I still get a little thrill. It is so cool to watch their brains open up and grasp ideas.

It doesn't have to be a monumental or unexpected task to make me proud. I get just as thrilled, probably even more, each time one of my children takes his first steps or puts her first string of words together in a coherent sentence. Sure, it's a natural and usually long-anticipated stage that children pass through, but it is still a monumental accomplishment.

Every change is a wonder. Every talent is a doorway to a yet-unseen world. Every moment of growth is recorded in my brain as a miracle.

⊞   ⊞   ⊞

Rupert is my sweetest child—not because this is the reality, but because he is the youngest and we have all voted on it and everyone agrees. He needs more sleep that most kids or he gets grumpy. He doesn't hurry when I want him to and can easily take a half an hour to brush his teeth while I am yelling, "Rupert what are you doing in there? If I can hear you singing, then you can't be brushing your teeth! We're going to miss the bus!" He sometimes struggles with listening to his teacher and sitting still in class. He can collect more garbage in his room—for his projects—than anyone else I've ever met in my entire life— including myself, and that's saying something. He is hypersensitive and doesn't handle teasing well.

He also tells me I'm the best mommy in the whole world and is full of "I love you!" words. He's snuggly. He draws amazing "maps" and complicated diagrams of his inventions. He lives in a world of wonder and discovery and is a little in awe of it himself. He often ponders aloud the possibilities that lie before him in his fantasy world, while I can only listen and enjoy. He tells his dad, "*I* don't think you're bald," because Rupert knows how it feels to be sensitive, and he projects that on others and is careful about their feelings. He hates to clean his room, but he longs to be helpful.

Yesterday morning, he left me a note under my pillow. It was a folded piece of paper with a heart shape cut out of it and magic marker words that said, "I love you, Mommy. Quack! Moo! Quack! Moo! I will do drobs."

Because, you see, Rupert hasn't yet learned to spell the word "jobs." It wasn't one of his spelling words this year, so he had to sound it out. As much as he loves new words, he doesn't always take time to pronounce the familiar ones correctly, and he sometimes runs more than one letter sound together. I suppose separating and enunciating is just too tedious for the more insignificant words when we all know what he means anyway.

He also has a darn cute lisp.

🔲 🔲 🔲

Rupert and Pandora can fight like cats and dogs, but within seconds, they can be laughing hysterically together. I'm usually either telling them to get along or to not get along so well and to calm down. I think they're probably okay and I'm the one who can't make up my mind.

How lucky my husband and I are to have these two "difficults," and how lucky they are to have us, really.

⊞ ⊞ ⊞

My older three children—my two adults and my teenager, Stanley, Otto, and Magnolia—have grown and changed so much in the last five years. That's what happens with "difficults." They change. Their good points sometimes change, and their difficult points also change, hopefully for the better as they refine and mature.

Magnolia's one goal in life used to be to get Otto in trouble. Ask her now and she'll tell you he's one of her best friends. She looks up to him. She needs him. He needs to be needed. He watches out for her and tries to help guide her through the tricky and turbulent teenage years. Now Stanley is in on the act. He said to me the other day, "You know, Magnolia's kind of a cool kid to have around."

My heart leaps when I hear these things, when I see so many of my children's strengths and weaknesses blend together with their quirks and mellow into something more beautiful than I could have ever anticipated. Are they perfect? Nope. Not even close. But they are pulling together to help each other make it through childhood and to grow up.

As the oldest child in the family, Stanley feels an obligation to be a good big brother. He *wants* to take care of his siblings. He *wants* relationships with each of them. He found Magnolia a job where he works, and he talked to the manager about arranging their schedules so that he can give her a ride as often as possible. He watches out for her while she's there. He reports back to her and me the nice things that people say about her. He also makes it a point to take each of his siblings out on "dates," which means dinner and a movie. He turned Rupert on to the

Teenage Mutant Ninja Turtles (oh, woe is me), which Stanley loved when he was Rupert's age.

☷ ☷ ☷

When I was growing up, my younger sister Gertrude really irritated me. She was the model child. If I wanted an extra piece of dessert and my mom said, "No, there isn't enough for seconds," then Gertrude would say, "She can have mine."

I ask you, how annoying is that? Especially when I knew I hadn't been nice to her and I really didn't deserve any kindness on her part. But as much as I despised her for her angelical generosity, I still took her up on her offer. I may have been greedy, but I was not stupid.

When I was in high school, I desperately wanted a boyfriend, but I was usually out of luck. Gertrude only rubbed salt in my wounds by wearing the ugliest polyester pantsuits this side of the seventies in sixth grade, and she still had admirers who gave her jewelry.

Now that we are all grown up, Gertrude is my best friend. She has helped me through the tough times. I can tell her anything. I know that when no one else understands, she will. That annoying little sister has turned out to be one of the most important people in my world.

I sometimes wonder: If my siblings and I didn't share a common growing up experience, if we didn't have so many years together, then would we get along as well as we do? I can't answer that question. I just know that something binds us in a way that is more powerful than embarrassment, anger, pride, thoughtlessness, and sorrow. As my dad often says, "It isn't over 'til it's over." We can't give up on each other.

I feel those same close ties with my children as they grow up and become adults. It is strange to watch them grow into my friends.

☷ ☷ ☷

I love looking at clouds. They can be so majestic, so overwhelming, so graceful. I love their colors and their shapes and the motions of them. They make me feel things that I don't know how to share with other people.

The other night, Hubby, Otto, and I were out driving around, and I was deep in thought about the clouds in the west and the purple blue of the darkening sky. We had another conversation going on, but I wasn't a full participant, as my mind was preoccupied by the clouds. A remark from Otto pulled me out of my reverie. "Mom, look at the clouds!"

Something in my heart leaped at that moment. There was someone else, a child of mine, who understood what I saw, what I felt. I knew I wasn't alone in my awe of the moment, and it felt good not to be alone, to know that someone else understood my emotional reaction to that sunset.

🈁 🈁 🈁

It isn't just blood that binds two souls. We can pull other people in, people we trust and understand, and we can form families beyond our own.

I remember when I was pregnant with Rupert. I was about six months along, and I was having one of those crazy, hormone-filled days. I was sad, and I didn't know why. When you're pregnant, you don't need a reason. Your emotions can just fly off in every direction without any consideration for anyone else. I was standing at the stove, stirring a pot of something, when Hubby came home. The poor guy had no idea what he was walking into.

I started crying. I felt pretty stupid about it, because I knew he was going to ask me what was wrong and I wouldn't be able to tell him, because I didn't have an answer. But he did something different this time. Without saying a word, he walked away from me and went over to the CD player and put on my favorite slow dance song. Then he came over to the stove and put his arms around me and we slow danced.

The tears ran freely down my face, but I felt comforted. That was all I needed. I didn't even know that I needed it, but he did.

Sometimes those close to you know you better than you know yourself. They can help you. They can be honest with you. They can encourage you. They can love you.

⊞　⊞　⊞

Everyone needs a support system. When you are gifted or "different" and you don't see things the same way other people do, and your mind goes off forever in another direction, and you just don't feel like you belong out there with the rest of the world—that someday they'll see through you, if they haven't already, and declare you an imposter, a faker, an alien from another planet— well, when you're different like that, it is such a relief to know that you have your own family to go back to, whether you're related by blood or some other invisible cord that binds you to a soul brother or soul sister. What a blessed relief to know that there are people who do know who you really are, good and bad, strengths and weaknesses, and they love you anyway.

This life is not always going to be an easy thing to navigate. Pulling together is vital. We may be the captains of our own destinies, but every one of us needs a crew to help guide the ship.

As parents, it is our duty to provide a home, a safe haven, where our children can know that they are loved and accepted for who they are, with or without their quirks and accomplishments. They need to be able to come home to us and to trust us. They don't need lectures, though they do need advice and they do need limits and boundaries. They want to be understood and supported in their giftedness and in every other positive aspect of their lives.

As for teachers, it is their responsibility to provide support in our classrooms. Children need to be allowed to express their giftedness rather than hiding it in shame or embarrassment. They need to know that you do understand why they are bored, that you do believe them when they say the "b" word. They need to be placed with peers who get their jokes and who can speak on their intellectual level. They should not have to grow up in a system that leaves them feeling forever like the odd man out.

As gifted adults, we must provide a network of kindred spirits and sanctuary for one another. We can't go it alone all of the time. We, too, need peers who understand us and who get our jokes. We need a shoulder to cry on every now and then. Pulling together with others, whether family or close friends, is a coping method, a strengthening tool that will get us through those times that seem impossible, and it will turn times of joy into times of great celebration.

Life in the fast brain can be a slightly bumpy ride, but I'm thoroughly enjoying the trip!

About the Author

Karen Isaacson is the author of the award-winning book *Raisin' Brains: Surviving My Smart Family* and co-author of *Intelligent Life in the Classroom: Smart Kids and Their Teachers*, which she wrote with Tamara Fisher. Karen has presented her humorous take on parenting gifted children at state and national conferences. She has five weird and wonderful gifted children who make every day unpredictable and who keep her on her toes and at the edge of her seat. In her spare time (which really exists only in an alternate reality), she pursues every creative endeavor she can get her hands on, while her left-brained husband patiently waits for her to get organized—someday. You can learn more about Karen at www.kisaacson.com.

Lightning Source UK Ltd.
Milton Keynes UK
UKHW021650170620
365158UK00005B/888